norma Gundersen

Homeward the Arrow's Flight

The Story of Susan La Flesche
[Dr. Susan La Fleche Picotte]

Revised Edition

Field Mouse
PRODUCTIONS
A Jean Lukesh Edition

Dr. Susan La Flesche Picotte, M.D., G.P.

Homeward the Arrow's Flight

The Story of
Susan La Flesche
[Dr. Susan La Flesche Picotte]

Revised Edition

MARION MARSH BROWN

Cover and Illustrations by
Ronald E. Lukesh

Field Mouse
PRODUCTIONS
Grand Island, Nebraska

Homeward the Arrow's Flight

Copyright © 1980 by Abingdon
Copyright © 1986 Marion Marsh Brown
Copyright © 1995 (rev. ed.) Marion Marsh Brown
Cover Art and Interior Art by Ronald E. Lukesh
Cover Photo—Medical College of Pennsylvania
Interior Photos—Nebraska State Historical Society
and the Medical College of Pennsylvania
Printed in the United States of America
by Record Printing Company, Cairo, Nebraska
Published by Field Mouse Productions
Grand Island, Nebraska
All rights reserved

Library of Congress Cataloging-in-Publication Data

BROWN, MARION MARSH, 1908–
Homeward the arrow's flight: The Story of Susan La Flesche
[Dr. Susan La Flesche Picotte] (revised edition)
"A Jean Lukesh Edition"—Half t.p.
SUMMARY: A biography of the young Omaha Indian
woman Susan La Flesche [Susan La Flesche Picotte] who
overcame sexual and cultural prejudices to become the first
Native American woman doctor of medicine. Revised
edition includes index, bibliography, list of family members,
and several photographs.
ISBN 0-9647586-0-1
1. Picotte, Susan La Flesche, 1865-1915–Juvenile literature.
2. La Flesche, Susan, 1865-1915–Juvenile literature. 3.
Physicians–Nebraska–Biography–Juvenile literature.   4.
Women physicians–Nebraska–Biography–Juvenile literature.
5. Omaha Indians–Biography–Juvenile literature.   [1.
Picotte, Susan La Flesche, 1865-1915. 2. La Flesche, Susan,
1865-1915. 3. Women physicians.   4.   Omaha Indians–
Biography.   5.   Indians of North America–Nebraska–
Biography.   6. Physicians] I. Title.
R154.L18B76   610'.92'4 [B] [92]
Library of Congress card number 95-61899   CIP

To all Native Americans who, like Susan La Flesche, have made a worthwhile contribution with their lives

Table of Contents

Susan La Flesche Picotte's Family

Joseph La Flesche (Iron Eye or Iron Eyes) (1818?-1888?)—Elected chief of the Omaha tribe; father of Louis, Francis, Susette, Rosalie, Marguerite, Susan, and five other children.

Mary Gale La Flesche (Hinnaugonun) (1826-1907)—One of Joseph La Flesche's wives; Susan's mother.

Nicomi (Nekomi)—Wife of Dr. John Gale; Mary Gale's mother; Susan's grandmother.

Louis La Flesche (1848-1860)—Son of Joseph La Flesche; brother of Susan La Flesche.

Susette La Flesche Tibbles (Bright Eye or Bright Eyes, Yosette or Josette) (1854-1903)—Reformer, writer, lecturer for Indian Rights; became famous as a result of the Trial of Standing Bear; Susan's oldest sister.

Thomas Tibbles (1840-1928)—Nebraska journalist; national advocate for Indian Rights; became famous as a result of the Trial of Standing Bear; ran for vice president on the People's Party ticket in 1904; husband of Susette LaFlesche; brother-in-law of Susan La Flesche.

Francis (Frank) La Flesche (1857-1932)—Anthropologist; writer; half-brother of Susan La Flesche; associate of anthropologist Alice Fletcher.

Rosalie La Flesche Farley (1861-1900)—Susan's sister.

Ed Farley—Rosalie's husband.

Marguerite La Flesche Picotte Diddock (1862-1945)—Teacher; Susan's sister.

Charles (Charlie) Picotte—Marguerite's first husband; brother of Henry Picotte.

Walter Diddock—Marguerite's second husband.

Susan La Flesche Picotte (1865-1915)—First Native American woman physician.

Henry (Henri) Picotte (d. 1905)—Susan's husband.

Caryl Picotte—Son of Henry and Susan La Flesche Picotte.

Pierre Picotte—Son of Henry and Susan La Flesche Picotte.

1

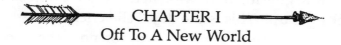

Susan half wakened, turned on her side, and opened her eyes. It was too early to get up. She plumped her pillow and closed her eyes again.

Suddenly a feeling of anticipation—of something exciting in the day ahead—flooded over her. What was it? Why, of course! She sat up in bed, hugging her knees. It was the day she and her sister Marguerite were to leave the reservation for school in the East.

Susan's thoughts raced back and forth between the life she knew on the Omaha Reservation in Nebraska and the unknown life to which she was going, a school called the Elizabeth Institute in Elizabeth, New Jersey. What would it be like to leave the place where she, though half white, had lived among Indians all of her fourteen years? Here she and Marguerite were respected as daughters of Joseph La Flesche, known to his people as Iron Eye, their last chief. At Elizabeth they would probably be known as "those strange Indian girls from the West."

Susan was proud of the La Flesche name. Her father had explained to her when she was small that it was French and meant "the Arrow." An arrow went straight and true—and often far—to its mark, she thought.

Marguerite had wakened. "Sue! Come on! Let's get up! This is the day!" she cried.

Susan jumped out of bed, for now the good smell of breakfast cooking came from below. She ran down the stairs but stopped suddenly in the kitchen doorway to watch her mother, who was impassive as always, cooking breakfast. Susan gazed at her thoughtfully, thinking that they would soon be separated. Her mother was a puzzle to her, yet a surge of love for her brought sudden tears very close.

After breakfast Susan and Marguerite finished packing. As they folded the last of their clothing, their older sister Rosalie came into the room, a billow of red-sprigged gray calico over her arm. "All done!" she announced, smiling at Susan.

"Oh, Ro, it's lovely!" Susan cried. "My traveling dress. How would we ever get along without you?"

"That's everything, isn't it?" Marguerite asked. "Let's see if we can close the trunk."

Marguerite dropped to her knees beside the trunk. Suddenly she looked up at her sister with big solemn black eyes. "Sue," she said, "I'm scared."

"Pooh!" Susan replied, silently telling her own fluttering heart to be still. The uncertainties that lay ahead were making her anxious too. But she wouldn't admit it. Although she was younger than Marguerite, she felt that she must take care of her. Marguerite was the most beautiful of the four La Flesche sisters, but she was also the most delicate and was often ill.

"Susette went East to school all by herself," Susan added. "I guess if she could do it alone, we can do it together."

Their father was a strong believer in education. He had seen, long before this year of 1879, that with the buffalo gone and the white settlers "coming like swarms of bees," as he put it, the Plains Indians had no alternative but to change the pattern of their lives. To that end, he was educating his children.

Marguerite sighed. "I still wish Rosalie were going instead of me," she said.

Suddenly Susette, the oldest La Flesche sister, appeared in the doorway. "Rosalie had her chance," she said sharply. "She has chosen to get married rather than educated."

Susan caught a hint of scorn in Susette's voice, and she started to spring to Rosalie's defense.

"Never mind, Little Sister," Rosalie said. She had joined them, having overheard the last of the conversation. "Susette has troubles of her own."

"Troubles? What troubles?" Susan demanded.

"Father has decided that she is to go with Standing Bear and Mr. Tibbles as interpreter on a lecture tour to win support for the Poncas."

Susan caught her breath. "Oh, Susette!" she cried, running to her.

It was unheard of among the Omahas that a maiden should associate in any way with men until a young brave came to court her. Many in the tribe would disapprove of her father's decision, but Iron Eye was not afraid of criticism. Susan knew well how his heart bled for their Ponca brothers, a tribe closely related to the Omahas.

The Poncas had been removed from their land in Nebraska to a hot, dry place in Oklahoma called Indian Territory, which they had dubbed the Land of the Red Dust. Unable to adjust to the heat and drought, a third of the tribe had died by year's end. Standing Bear and a handful of others had left the new reservation to return the bones of their dead to the old hunting grounds in Nebraska for burial.

Susan well remembered the day they had arrived at her father's door the previous spring, ragged and half-starved after their fifteen hundred mile trek. Even more vivid in her memory was the day shortly thereafter when army officers arrived and arrested the Poncas for leaving without the permission of the reservation agent.

The Poncas had then been driven off the Omaha Reservation like cattle. Susan could still remember how her father's jaw had set so he would not say angry words.

"Where are they taking them?" she had cried.

"To Omaha City—seventy long miles away."

When news came that Standing Bear and other leaders had been imprisoned, Iron Eye and his oldest daughter Susette had gone to see if they could help. Upon their return they had much to report. Concerned citizens in Omaha City had petitioned for the release of the prisoners, but to no avail. Then two important lawyers and a newspaperman named Thomas Tibbles had taken their plight to court. The government had contended that the Indians could not be heard in court because "Indians were not people."

When her father had reached this point in his account, Susan had burst out, "Indians aren't *people!* Then what *are* we?"

"Patience, Daughter," her father had admonished, rubbing his thigh above the wooden leg he wore. "Judge Dundy is a good and honest man. His decision disputed this foolish contention. He ruled in favor of the Indians. 'The Indian *is* a person,' Judge Dundy has said."

So the Poncas had been released, but because their lands in Nebraska had not been restored to them, Mr. Tibbles was attempting to stir up sentiment in their favor, first through the columns of his newspaper, and now through

7

the proposed lecture tour.

Susan knew that to follow her father's wishes and set off with Standing Bear and Mr. Tibbles would be very difficult for Susette. Impulsively, Susan hugged her older sister. Both of them would be leaving home soon, but for different reasons.

Soon their father was at the door with the team hitched to the spring wagon, and last-minute excitement took over. They climbed into the wagon, their skirts billowing over the plank seat.

"Good-bye!"

"Good-bye! Don't forget to write," Rosalie called.

Only Susette and their father were going to the train station with Susan and Marguerite. Susette had been East before and knew about buying tickets and getting on trains.

Susan looked back at the little group standing beside the porch: her grandmother Nicomi; her mother Mary; her sister Rosalie. She had to blink hard to see them, for her eyes were filled with tears. But for their sakes she smiled, and, as long as she could see them, she continued to wave her handkerchief.

When they were no longer in sight, Susan dried her eyes and concentrated on absorbing every detail of the landscape. All of this that she was leaving she must carry with her in memory. She peered into the woods that were just beginning to show dapples of red and burnished gold. She gazed over the hills to the winding river below. She loved every inch of this country.

All too soon they reached the little maroon depot framed with its platform of bricks. Their father tied the horses to the hitching post behind the building, as far as possible from where the train would come roaring down the track, and the girls clambered down from the wagon.

"Come with me," Susette said. Marguerite and Susan followed to the ticket window.

Susette purchased the tickets and thrust one of them into Susan's hand. "Put this in your purse, and don't lose it. The conductor will ask for it soon after the train has started."

Susan nodded dumbly. The sharp whistle of the approaching train pierced her consciousness. Under her feet she felt the vibration of the black, belching monster as it clanged and clattered to a stop.

She found her voice when she felt her father's hand on her arm. "Good-bye, Father."

"You learn well," he said.

Susette pushed them up the steps, and then Susan realized: She was on a train! The excitement of the new adventure took over, and she was surprised to see that Marguerite was crying.

"All aboard!" resounded through the car,

and Susan felt goose pimples break out on her arms. She leaned across Marguerite and peered through the smoke-darkened window to wave good-bye.

With a great hissing of steam, they were off, the depot and the little figures on the platform disappearing in the distance. Now it was up to them, Susan thought—two half-Indian girls going into an all-white world. The thought that surfaced from among the many that were churning in her mind was: "We are La Flesches. We can do it."

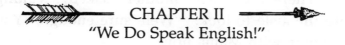
"We Do Speak English!"

During the first few hours of the trip, the knowledge that they must change trains in Lincoln filled Susan with foreboding. Once they had negotiated the change, however, she and Marguerite relaxed.

"I don't know why I was so scared," Susan said with a sigh as they settled themselves in another green plush double seat.

Marguerite was burrowing into their food basket. "I know," she said. "Weren't we silly?"

"Anyway, that's over, and now I'm starved."

Marguerite handed her some jerked beef.

"Mmmmm, good!" Susan exclaimed with relish, remembering how she had helped her mother and Rosalie dry the thin strips of meat during the summer.

As they chewed on the jerky, Susan looked around her. The people on this train were well dressed. "Stylish," she said to Marguerite. She could see no other Indians. "We're already in another world," she thought.

A little girl went by to get a drink. She stared at Marguerite and Susan. When she had returned to her seat, Susan heard her say, "Mama, there are Indians back there!"

"There are?" her mother asked, leaning into the aisle to look. "Well, sure enough! You stay here with Mama now."

Susan looked at Marguerite, and they giggled.

"I s'pose she thinks we're savages," Marguerite said, laughing.

The train lumbered on in the deepening dark, and looking out the window was no longer rewarding. Susan's eyes were getting heavier and heavier. She tossed a shawl over her sister then covered herself. Almost instantly she was asleep.

Later, when the train lurched to a stop at a station, she wakened with a start. Where was she? What was happening? She had been dreaming about her brother Louis—the brother she had never seen. She sat up, blinking, and saw a little depot silhouetted against the stream of floodlight. Then she remembered where she was.

As the train moved out, she lay back down and thought about the dream she had just had—and the story of Louis, which she had heard so often from Susette.

Long before Susan's birth, her mother and father had gone to visit friends in the Pawnee tribe. While they were away, their son Louis had become ill. Louis was their first-born and a fine lad of twelve. As the parents were coming home, they were met by a runner sent to tell them to make haste because Louis was very ill. By the time they reached home, Louis was dead.

Cowering in the woodbox behind the cookstove, sister Susette had watched as her father came in, carrying the body of her brother. Grandmother Nicomi found her there and carried her upstairs to bed. Nicomi said afterward that her father held Louis' body all night. But by the time Susette awoke the next morning, they had put Louis in a little wooden box.

Susan could feel the tears welling in her eyes, just remembering Susette's account.

"He should never have died." That was the way Susette had always ended the story.

As Susan drifted back to sleep, she thought about the two tragedies that had occurred in her family because of the lack of medical facilities on the reservation: Louis' death and her father's loss of his leg because of an infection. Maybe... maybe.... Just the faint glimmer of an idea found its way into her sleep-fogged brain. Could *she* possibly serve her people by becoming a nurse? But the regular rhythm of the wheels on the tracks was singing a lullaby, and again she slept. The next time she wakened, it was to daylight and trees flashing by the window.

As the day wore on, Susan began to think their journey would never end. Her eyes ached from peering out the window. The monotonous sound of the clanking wheels and the sight of the moving landscape seemed to dull her brain. The only time she could rouse herself was when the train pulled into a station. Then there was the excitement of the scene on the platform below: the loading and unloading of freight and baggage and the loading and unloading of passengers.

It was growing dusk when the conductor stopped by and said, "Elizabeth's the next stop."

They watched the lights of Elizabeth come into view, and Susan's heart began to pound. By the time the conductor called, "Elizabeth! Elizabeth, New Jersey!" the pounding seemed to fill her whole chest, nearly stifling her.

"Oh, dear, I do hope Miss Read or Miss Higgins will be there to meet us," Marguerite said.

The train screeched to a halt, and they were in the crowd of people moving toward the door. As they stood at the top of the steps, Susan scanned the faces on the platform. How would they know Miss Read or Miss Higgins? Susette had said something about Miss Higgins wearing nose-pinching glasses and wearing her hair in a bun. Suddenly Susan spied two women, straight-backed and very neatly dressed, standing at the foot of the steps, looking up and smiling directly at her and Marguerite.

"There they are!" she cried.

As the girls reached the bottom of the train steps, a soft voice said, "You must be Susan. And you're Marguerite. How good to see you."

A small gloved hand reached out to Susan, and she found that she could breathe again. Her lively spirit asserted itself at once.

"Now let *me* guess," Susan said with a little giggle. "*You're* Miss Higgins, and *you're* Miss Read!"

Her guess proved correct, and, though she felt a bit ill at ease in the presence of the two dignified women, she was glad to be in their care.

"We'll just see to your trunk," Miss Higgins said. "Then we'll catch the trolley."

Susan was eager to see a trolley. Susette had told them it was something like a train but that it was pulled by horses and ran on tracks right down the middle of the street.

"There comes our car," Miss Read said as a trolley came clattering down the street.

"This way," Miss Higgins said, helping the girls up the step and onto a platform where she jingled coins into a strange-looking container.

"Let's move back," Miss Read said, leading

the way as the car suddenly lurched forward.

Soon the trolley stopped—with almost as much of a jolt as when it had started. Riding a trolley car was dangerous business! Susan was glad when they were on firm ground again.

Now they were in front of a large house, and Miss Read and Marguerite were turning in at the gate.

"Well, here we are," Miss Higgins said cheerfully.

"You mean this—this—"

"This is Elizabeth Institute."

Susan stared at the tall house with its many windows and cupolas, its pillared front verandah, and its big brick chimneys.

"Do you like it?" Miss Higgins asked, smiling at the rapt look on Susan's face.

"Oh, it's—it's *beautiful!*" Susan breathed.

"Come along now. We're already late for dinner."

When they were inside, Miss Higgins led them into a room and said, "Just come in here and leave your things."

Susan thought it was very quiet. Where were all the girls? She looked about her at the beautiful room they had entered, feeling the thick carpeting under her feet.

"You can wash here," Miss Higgins said, indicating a pitcher and bowl.

"Where are the girls?" Susan asked.

"They're at dinner now. You'll see them in a minute. The dormitories are upstairs. We'll take you up after we've eaten."

"Are you ready?" Miss Read asked from the doorway.

Susan saw that Marguerite too had removed her bonnet and smoothed her hair and had, no doubt, washed her hands.

The four of them moved along a corridor, down a flight of steps, and to the open door of a large room filled with round tables at which girls were seated. Every girl's eyes were riveted on the new arrivals. Susan could feel Marguerite shrink back at the sight. She punched her sister, straightened to her full height, and stared back defiantly at the staring sea of faces.

"Girls," Miss Read said, "we have two new pupils, the La Flesche sisters. This is Susan, and this is Marguerite."

The girls at the tables nodded politely and began to eat again, a quiet buzz of conversation following the dead silence that had greeted the strangers' appearance.

"We've assigned you to this table," Miss Read said, leading the way to the middle of the room. "Susan and Marguerite, this is Mary Ann Beiton; this is Jane Trumbull...."

Susan's mind became a , .ble of names and faces. She inclined her head slightly at each introduction, as she had seen the others do, and noticed that Marguerite was doing the same. Miss Read indicated the two vacant chairs at the table, and Susan slipped into one.

Conversation broke out at the table. Everyone was talking, it seemed, except the two newcomers. In fact, Susan thought, they were talking as if she and Marguerite were not there.

"I'd *heard* they were going to take a couple of Indians, but I didn't believe it," Susan heard one girl say.

"They're from way out West, I heard, where it isn't civilized at all."

"Their hair's pretty and shiny, isn't it?"

"And so *black!*"

Then Susan could scarcely believe her ears at the next remark.

"I wonder how long it will take them to learn English."

Susan looked in surprise at the girl who had spoken. Marguerite had evidently heard too, for Susan heard a small giggle at her side. It was too much. Susan broke into uncontrollable laughter, her hands over her face.

"She isn't crying, is she?" she heard someone ask, and at this she laughed all the harder.

"Shhh!" Marguerite whispered, but Susan knew that she was laughing too.

Susan removed her hands from her face, wiped her eyes on her sleeve, and said to the staring girls, "We do speak English, of course."

There was a chorus of "You *do*?" then other choruses of "Oh, not really!" and "We're sorry." But as the others saw that Susan and Marguerite were only amused at their mistake, they began to laugh too.

"My, you girls are having a good time," said Miss Higgins, coming to stand beside the table as the laughter subsided quickly. "If you are through with your dinner," she added to Susan and Marguerite, "I will take you upstairs and show you your quarters."

They went upstairs and were conducted into a large room that contained a number of narrow beds. Between each two beds stood a tall piece of furniture with two doors, below which were drawers. Miss Higgins led the girls across the room to where their small horsehair trunk stood between two beds.

"These will be your beds," she said, "and this," pointing to the piece between them, "is your wardrobe. You will want to get unpacked, so I'll leave you. All lights go out at nine. That's curfew."

Suddenly Susan was very tired, and the beds

looked extremely inviting. "Let's hurry and get unpacked," she said. "Maybe we can get into bed before the other girls come up. Somehow I don't feel up to any more of them tonight."

They hung their dresses in the wardrobe and put their other things in the drawers. Susan crossed the room and stood looking out the window. She could hear the clop-clop of horses' hoofs on the pavement. It made her think of her pony named Pie, and all at once she was desperately homesick.

"Sue, hurry up! Get into bed," Marguerite hissed. "The girls are coming."

Susan slipped quickly into her bed. "Pretend to be asleep," she whispered.

She turned her face into the pillow. The tears were very close, and, just in case some curious stranger came peering, she did not want to be caught crying should the tears spill over.

Getting started in classes the next day left little time for thinking about home. It seemed to Susan that she was no more issued a book for one class than they had moved on to another. First there was grammar and composition, with an assignment to write a paper. Next were the reading books and then a book called *Physiology and Hygiene*. Fascinated, Susan thumbed through the pages, looking at the pictures and diagrams of the parts of the human body.

Even with all the excitement of classwork, it was soon obvious to Susan that her sister, as usual, was getting the lion's share of attention.

"Oh, Marguerite!" one of the girls would exclaim. "Your eyes are so beautiful! I'll bet you really have the boys at your feet."

"At my feet?" Marguerite would ask, puzzled.

Laughter would follow. "Beaus. You know—boyfriends. Don't you have lots of boyfriends back home?"

Demurely Marguerite would reply, "We Indians do not have beaus. One day a young man will come ask Father's permission, and we will be married."

Susan wished the girls would ask her the kind of questions they asked Marguerite. She looked at herself in the mirror. Her hair was exactly like her sister's. Her eyes were the same color, but they didn't have the dreamy, smoldering look of Marguerite's. She had to admit that the oval shape of her sister's face, with a pointed chin, was more attractive than her round one.

Well, enough of feeling sorry for herself, Susan decided. "I'm going down to the library to study," she said to Marguerite. "Aren't you coming?"

"No. Who wants to study all the time?" Marguerite replied, flopping down on the bed.

"Nobody that I know of. But you'd better do more than you're doing or you won't even pass."

"You don't need to tell me what to do. I'm older than you are. If anybody is going to tell anybody, *I'll* tell *you*."

"All right, if you want to fail and get sent home."

Susan picked up her books and went out of the room. She had just reached the library door when she heard Miss Read call her name.

"Will you please come here a minute, Susan? There's a letter here for you and Marguerite."

News from home! Susan was so excited that she forgot all about studying. Letter in hand, she hurried back up the stairs to Marguerite, forcing herself not to run, because running was not allowed at Elizabeth.

"Marg! Marg! We have a letter from Ro!" She dropped down on the bed beside Marguerite. Hurriedly, she tore open the envelope. With heads together, the girls pored lovingly over the letter.

The rest of the day Susan could think of nothing but the letter and its news from home. When she tried to study, she would see a passage in Ro's handwriting, instead of the printed words on the page before her. Then she would be back on the reservation with her dear ones.

Grandmother Nicomi had been sick with a bad cold, Ro had written. Their mother had boiled jimson weed and made poultices for her chest, and she was better now. Susette had left for Washington, D. C. The rest of them were well. They had dug potatoes and brought in the pumpkins, for it might freeze any time now.

Susan lived it all with them. There was only one class that day that could take her mind from thoughts of home. That was her physiology class. They were studying the circulatory system, and it was captivating. She enjoyed learning how the valves of the heart opened and closed, how the arteries carried the blood from the heart, and how the veins carried it back. She'd had no idea what a system of branching roadways extended through a person's body!

But she went to bed that night thinking about home rather than physiology. Her eyes ached for the sight of a red-orange Nebraska sunset. Her hand ached for the soft touch of her pony's nose. Her mind throbbed with homesickness, and she cried herself to sleep.

Susan awakened early, long before the other girls were stirring. All her life she had been accustomed to rising early. As she rose up on her elbow, she could see that her sister still slept. Marguerite seemed to welcome the opportunity to sleep longer. Susan sighed, punched her pillow, turned over, and closed her eyes. But it was no use; she was wide awake.

Then she heard a sound she had come to listen for each morning: the clop-clop of a horse's hoofs on the cobbled street below. It was the milkman on his rounds, delivering his bottles of milk while the city still slept. The first time she had heard the sound, she had jumped from her bed and run to the window. She had thought it very funny to see the milk for their breakfast porridge coming to the house this way.

As she listened to the welcome hoofbeats coming closer, the surge of homesickness returned. How she longed to have Pie nuzzle her hand! Suddenly she threw back the covers, slipped out of bed, and dressed hurriedly. She threw her shawl around her shoulders and crept down the stairs. She had to go past Miss Read's room to reach the front door, and, horror of horrors, a gleam of light shone under the headmistress' door. She was already up! Susan scarcely breathed as she tiptoed by. She reached the heavy door with its lock and key. If she could open it without arousing anyone, she would be safe.

As she turned the big key, she thought the grating sound it made could surely be heard all over the house. With her heart beating hard, she pulled gently on the doorknob. The door did not budge. She pulled harder. Suddenly it gave way and flew open, pushing her against the wall. She held her breath, listening for Miss Read's door to open. But when she heard nothing, she slipped out, noiselessly pulling the door shut behind her.

The world was bathed in predawn shadows, but she could tell that the horse and cart were no longer in front of Elizabeth Institute. She hurried through the gate and ran pell-mell down the street. It was a glorious feeling to be running out in the cold early morning air. She let her shawl fly loose, thinking she must look like a big bat swooping through the semidarkness.

The big houses in this part of the city were set far apart and surrounded by park-like lawns. It wasn't until she was approaching the second house beyond the Institute that Susan again heard the clop-clop that had called her from bed. Then the sound ceased, and she slowed her steps.

The milkman had stopped. He jumped from his high seat, grabbed his carrier of milk, and ran up the walk. This was Susan's chance. She began speaking quietly to the horse as she approached, and its big head turned toward her. Susan reached up and touched the head lightly, then stroked it caressingly. "Nice horse. What's your name? Do you like getting out so early in the morning?"

She had just put her hand under the horse's nose, wishing she had a carrot, when a big voice at her elbow said, "What's this? A girl? What are you doing here?"

Susan jumped. "Oh, I—I was just petting your horse."

"I see. But where did you come from?"

Susan gestured down the street. "The Institute," she said.

"Well, you'd better be getting back before they miss you." The man sounded very surprised, but amused too.

"Oh—Oh, I guess that's right." She felt she owed the man an explanation. "I just *had* to feel a horse's muzzle. You see, it's been a month since..."

The milkman was back in his cart and lifting the reins. "You got a horse back home?" he asked in sudden understanding.

"Yes," Susan called as the cart moved off, "a pony named Pie."

She turned slowly back toward the Institute. It had been wonderful, this brief respite from regimentation, this brief moment of freedom. She smiled, remembering the feel of the horse's head and of its soft nose, the nostrils breathing in and out, searching her palm. She would slip some of those funny little sugar cubes, the likes of which she'd never seen before, from the table into her pocket. Then the next time.... She began to skip.

Suddenly a large form loomed directly in her path. Startled, she looked up and saw that it was a policeman, legs spraddled and arms outstretched to block her. In one hand he held his club.

"Aha! he said. "So here you are! Is your name Susan La Flesche?" He peered into her face.

"Y—yes," Susan stammered.

"What do you mean runnin' away like this and causin' a peck of trouble?"

"But I'm not running away," Susan protested, her chin up. Nevertheless, she began to tremble. They had missed her and had thought she'd run away! They'd even called the police! Oh, dear! Now she supposed she was in for it.

The policeman had her by the arm, propelling her rapidly and none too gently down the street. "I'll just deliver you right into the hands of the good ladies at the Institute.

Causin' all this trouble and scarin' 'em to death!"

"But I was on my way back!" Susan insisted.

It was growing light now, and as they approached the fenced-in yard of the Institute, Susan realized that there was a great deal more clatter and clamor about the school than usual. "I'll bet I really *am* in for it!" she thought.

CHAPTER IV
A Visit From Home

The policeman pushed through the gate and bellowed, "Here she is! Here's your runaway!"

The next minute Susan was surrounded by girls. Marguerite, sobbing, threw her arms around her, almost choking her. Down the verandah steps came Miss Read and Miss Higgins. The policeman held Susan's arm until the ladies reached them.

"I'll turn her over to you this time," he said threateningly as he released her. "But there'd better not be a next time." He moved toward the gate mumbling, "Causin' all this trouble..."

"Oh, Susan!" Marguerite sobbed. "Don't you know I couldn't get along without you? When I woke up and saw you were gone..."

So that was it. Marguerite had sounded the alarm.

"All right, Marguerite. Let's just let Susan come in and tell her story," Miss Read said.

"And all the rest of you girls get back in and be ready for breakfast when the bell rings," Miss Higgins said sternly.

Susan did not say a word. With Miss Read at her side and Marguerite still clinging to her, she walked into the house. Although she was still trembling, her lips were pressed tightly together. She hadn't done anything so terrible!

And she wasn't about to say she had.

Breakfast was over, and the girls were trooping back up the stairs by the time Susan had finished telling Miss Read her story. She was surprised when the headmistress said, "Go down, and tell the cook to give you your breakfast," but she did as she was told. So it was not until Latin class that she saw Marguerite again.

"What did she do to you?" Marguerite whispered.

"Nothing," Susan said. Then, knowing Marguerite's concern, she wrote in her notebook where her sister could see. "I didn't run away. I just went out to pet the milkman's horse."

Between classes, she whispered to Marguerite, "Miss Read just told me it was against the rules to leave the school without permission—and that no lady went out alone."

"Isn't she going to punish you?"

"I'm not allowed to go to town Saturday. That's all."

The Saturday shopping excursions were keenly anticipated by most of the girls, but not by Marguerite and Susan, who had no money to spend. So Susan was not concerned about her punishment. She even wondered if Miss Read hadn't meted it out with perfect understanding, for she was sure she had detected a twinkle in the headmistress' eye as she told her story.

One day shortly after her escapade, Susan

and Marguerite were both called into Miss Read's apartment.

"She's probably going to tell me I'm failing Latin," Marguerite said dispiritedly.

But Miss Read was not wearing her scolding face. She was smiling when the girls entered.

"I have splendid news for you," she said. "Your sister Susette is coming to visit."

"Here? Susette's coming *here*?" Susan cried.

"Oh, when?" Marguerite asked eagerly.

"She will be here tomorrow, and she plans to stay overnight."

"How wonderful!" exclaimed Susan.

"We are proud to claim her as one of our graduates" Miss Read said, "and we will be very happy to have her here. The newspapers report that she is doing a splendid job of interpreting the Indians' problems to the people in the East. And the accounts all speak of her poise and presence on the lecture platform."

Susan nodded. She and Marguerite had seen some of the accounts. They had high praise for Bright Eyes. (Bright Eyes was the English translation of Susette's Indian name. Reporters had picked this up, and Susette was now being billed as Bright Eyes.)

There was one aspect of their sister's visit, however, that Susan hadn't counted on. Susette arrived just before dinner time, and, when she was escorted into the dining hall by Miss Read and Miss Higgins, with Marguerite and Susan following, there was a stir among the girls.

Miss Read rang her little bell for silence. "Girls," she said, "I want you to meet our very honored guest, Susette La Flesche. She is the sister of Marguerite and Susan, and she is a graduate of our school. She is on a lecture tour at present, and some of you may have seen her picture in the papers. We are very proud to claim her and happy to have her visiting us."

Susette was stylishly dressed and looked the part that she now played. There was no doubt that the girls were impressed. By bedtime neither was there any doubt that Marguerite's and Susan's social standing had risen sharply as well.

To Susan the best part of Susette's visit was hearing about home, for it was not long since she had left the reservation.

"Did Nicomi get over the cold on her lungs?" she wanted to know.

"Yes," Susette replied, "Nicomi's all right again. But Mother's been sick."

"Somebody's *always* sick," Susan said unhappily.

"They don't take care of themselves," Susette answered.

"I know. And I don't think they get the right things to eat. I never thought about it until we came here. But tell us about Ro and her wedding plans. Oh, Susette, can't we please go home for the wedding?" Susan begged.

"Please say we can!" Marguerite chimed in.

"No, you most certainly cannot. In the first place, there's no money for railroad fare. In the second place, you can't leave your studies."

"But *you* have money to travel around on. Can't you let us have a little of yours?" Marguerite said, pouting.

"We could take our books and study on the train. I'm sure I could keep up, and I'd help Marguerite. Please, Susette!"

"No! I said 'no,' and that's final. As for 'my' money, it isn't mine. You know that. It's furnished to me by the Connecticut Indian Fund and the Presbyterian Mission, and it's only for my work."

Susan sighed.

"If you think *you* should go home," Susette went on, "what do you think about poor Mr. Tibbles? He received word that his wife had died back in Nebraska, and he didn't even leave the tour to go home for her burial."

"Well, I think that was terrible!" Susan cried. "I think families should be together for weddings and funerals."

"No matter what you think," replied Susette, "you can't go home for Ro's wedding."

Susan saw that further pleading was useless. "I *would* have liked to see Ro in her wedding dress," she said dreamily. "And Ed all dressed up. Do you mind that she isn't marrying an Indian, Susette?"

33

"Of course not. Ed Farley is a hard-working, reliable young man, and I think he will make Ro a very good husband."

"And Ro loves him," Marguerite put in.

"After all, two of our grandparents married whites," Susette said.

Susan smiled at the foolishness of her question. And yet if she were ever to marry, she felt it would be right for her to marry an Indian.

Marguerite and Susan were excused from classes on the day that Susette spent with them, and this too gave them prestige. It was a great day, not only for those reasons, but because Susette's presence had brought home very close. Susan decided that this closeness was the best thing that had come from her visit. The worst was the attitude Susette's visit imposed on the part of the Misses Read and Higgins. From that day forward, it seemed to Susan, the ladies were forever implying that she and Marguerite should follow in Susette's footsteps. Wasn't it enough that they were following her in attending Elizabeth Institute? Couldn't it end there? Susan was sure she did not want to become a lecturer. What bothered her was that she did not know what she did want to become.

CHAPTER V

Susan Takes the Blame

"Sue, I feel sick. I don't think I'll get up for breakfast." Marguerite's voice came weakly from the bed next to Susan's.

Susan's mind worked quickly. "Hmmm. I wonder," she thought. She jumped out of bed and put her hand on Marguerite's forehead. "You don't have any fever," she said. "Are you sure it isn't because examinations start today that you're feeling sick?"

There was no answer.

"Marg, it's no good. If you don't take the tests today, you'll just have to take them another day."

This time there was a sigh from the other bed. Then the covers were heaved off, and Marguerite said, "I hate examinations! I'm so *scared*. I really do feel sick, Sue."

Susan felt a stab of compassion. She didn't mind examinations at all. In fact, they were a challenge. But she realized that for Marguerite it wasn't that way at all.

"I'm sorry," she said. "Is it Latin you're worried about? If we hurry, I'd have time to hear your declensions. Maybe that would help."

When the two days of examinations were over, there was a short break before the second term. The girls who lived close enough went home for the interim, and for those who were left there was a holiday feeling. No lessons to do! No routine of classes to follow.

"Just freedom!" Susan said to Marguerite. "But freedom within these walls, and what's there to do here?"

One afternoon as Susan was looking for a book in the library, Miss Higgins called to her. "Susan," she said, "how would you like to take drawing next term?"

Susan looked doubtful. "I don't know if I can draw."

"I thought you might enjoy it. You seem to have more than ample time to master your regular subjects, so, if you wish, you may add drawing."

"All right," Susan said. "I'll try."

Miss Higgins smiled and said. "That's one of your assets, Susan. You're always willing to try."

The weather was cold, and there was a definite hint of snow in the air. When Miss Read and Miss Higgins took the girls for a walk in the afternoon, Susan said, with her nose to the sky, "I smell snow."

The other girls laughed, but, sure enough, by dusk snow was falling. Susan pressed her face to the windowpane, longing to be out in it. By nightfall the ground was covered with a thick, fluffy white blanket.

"I wish we could go coasting," Susan said to the other girls as they sat in front of the library fireplace.

"Not a chance," said Eleanor, a pretty redhead from upper New York. "They'd never let us."

Susan caught a note of longing in her voice. "I'll bet you go coasting where you come from," she said.

Eleanor nodded. "And sleighing. My father has a cutter sleigh, and it's all we ride in, in winter."

"Do you have sleighbells?" Susan asked.

"Oh, yes, and when we go jingling down the road, it's—oh, it's beautiful. I love winter at home."

"She's homesick," Susan thought. Well, why couldn't they go coasting and have a little fun before they went back to lessons?

"We could ask," Eleanor said thoughtfully.

"But we don't have a sled," Marguerite put in sensibly.

Susan's nimble mind was jumping around like a young colt let out to pasture. "Marg," she said, "remember when some of the children who didn't have a sled brought an old bread pan to the hill?"

Marguerite began to laugh. "Oh, yes! And how they spun 'round and 'round going down the hill, yelling like..."

"Like Indians?" Jane Trumbull laughed.

Jane was a plump, jolly girl whose sense of humor appealed to Susan. Everyone laughed at her remark, Susan and Marguerite with the others. Suddenly Susan realized that she no longer felt different among the other girls. She and Marguerite had been accepted.

But the thoughts that were tingling in her brain had to do with coasting. "They must have big pans here to mix bread in. They'd have to, for all the bread they bake."

"Susan La Flesche, what are you thinking?" demanded Eleanor, her eyes dancing.

"You know what I'm thinking."

"But they wouldn't let us have one," said Aretha Stone, a mousy little girl whom Susan had pegged in her mind as a 'fraidy cat.

"No-o-o," Susan said thoughtfully, "I suppose not."

"And even if they did, Miss Read would never let us go coasting," Marguerite said. "She's so cautious. She'd be sure to say, 'Oh, no, I couldn't. It would be too dangerous. After all, Miss Higgins and I are responsible for you girls.'"

They all laughed at Marguerite's clever mimicry.

Then Susan said in a low voice, "I wasn't thinking of asking her."

There was a little gasp from the circle of girls, followed by excited chatter.

"Shhh!" Susan cautioned. "Let's sleep on

it."

There was a good deal of whispering after the girls went to bed that night. The next morning, the minute Susan awoke, she ran to the window. Yes, there had been more snow, but the storm seemed to be over.

As they were leaving the dining hall after breakfast, Susan approached Miss Higgins. "Marguerite and I don't have anything to do," she said. "Could we go to the kitchen and offer to help Cook?"

Miss Higgins looked surprised. She blinked her eyes a couple of times, then said, "Why, yes, I suppose so."

The cook seemed pleased to have them. With only a few girls left to cook for, she was alone in the kitchen. She was a buxom German woman who plunged her big arms into the dishwater with the same vigor she applied to beating a cake. She asked her helpers to begin drying silver and glassware.

Susan pulled open a cupboard door. "Is this where the glasses go?" she asked.

"Not down there," said the cook. "That's for pots and pans. Glasses up here."

"Oh," Susan said with a frown. "I wouldn't think your pots-and-pans cupboard would be big enough to hold bread pans. Don't you mix your bread in great big pans?" She put out her arms to demonstrate the size.

"Ya, they're too big. They hang in the

pantry." She gave a nod of her head toward the pantry.

"Oh, I see," Susan said, strolling innocently in that direction. There was no door between pantry and kitchen, and she saw at once what she had come for. She also saw that Marguerite was having difficulty keeping her face straight. So she said, "Well, thanks for letting us help. We'll come in again and see if there's anything we can do. Do you work all afternoon?"

"Na, I get a nap after lunch."

"Oh, that's good," Susan replied. "After the lunch dishes are done."

"Ya."

Now Susan had all she needed to know.

"You hypocrite!" Marguerite giggled as they left. "You can't fool me. You've got a scheme."

Susan nodded. She had it all thought out, but she wasn't going to confide in the others.

"That hill in the park's a good one," Marguerite said.

Susan smiled. That was the hill all right. But first she would have to borrow the bread pans during cook's naptime, and then later that night they would have to get outside. She'd made it out the front door once without arousing Miss Read or Miss Higgins, but she had been alone then. Could she do it with a half dozen followers?

After bedtime inspection, when all seemed quiet below stairs, the other girls tiptoed into the room with Marguerite and Susan, and Susan divulged her plan.

We must be sure the ladies are asleep before we try to sneak outside," Susan said.

"Somebody can slip down and report when their lights are out," Jane suggested.

"Good. How about you?"

Jane nodded.

"Now be sure you dress good and warm."

The girls waited nearly an hour after lights were out in the schoolmistresses' rooms. Then, bundled up to their chins, the six slipped noiselessly down the stairs and reached the front door without making a sound. Holding her breath, Susan turned the key and pulled open the door. No trouble this time! One by one the girls filed out, carrying the bread pans.

Once they reached the park, however, their high spirits erupted like a volcano.

"Oh, it'll be perfect!" Susan cried. "Who wants to go first?"

"You get first turn," they chorused.

"Without you, we'd never be here," Jane said stoutly.

"Well, there are two pans. Who wants the other one?"

"I do!" Eleanor cried.

"Here I go!" shouted Susan.

As she went whirling around and around, gaining momentum with every second of her downward plunge, her shouts rang out on the crisp night air—no screams of fright, but sounds of pure joy—a free spirit reveling in freedom.

She and Eleanor plodded back up the hill carrying the big round pans that had spun them down the hill like tops.

"Who's next?"

"Watch out for that tree at the bottom, on your left."

Soon they had had three turns each, except for Aretha who had had none. Now the girls were urging her to try it at least once.

"Doesn't it make you dizzy?" she asked.

"Sure. That's part of the fun."

"No, I don't think I'll go."

"Oh, Aretha, it's so much fun! Come on. Don't be a 'fraidy cat."

"Don't urge her if she doesn't want to go," Susan said.

But the challenge had done its work. "I guess I'll go just once," Aretha said weakly.

"Then I think we'd better get back," Susan advised.

"So do I," said Marguerite. "I'm freezing."

"Susan, will you go ahead of me?" Aretha asked.

Susan took off down the hill. Every time the pan spun, she could see another whirling dervish plummeting after her, but she heard no sound from it. "She's scared dumb," she thought. "They really shouldn't have urged her to go."

In an instant Susan was at the bottom, picking herself up out of the snow. But where was Aretha? She should have been right beside her. Then she saw, and her heart stood still. Aretha had done the one thing that all the others had avoided: She had spun left, directly into the tree. Now she lay sprawled beside it. As Susan ran to her side, the other girl made no effort to get up.

"Aretha! Aretha! Are you hurt?"

A little moan answered her. Susan put her arms under the injured girl's shoulders and held her. "Aretha! Where are you hurt?"

All at once Aretha seemed to become fully conscious. "My leg!" she screamed.

Seeing that something was wrong, the other girls came running down the hill. "What's the matter? What happened?"

"I'm afraid she's broken her leg," Susan said calmly. "Marguerite, make a carryall with me." Marguerite stretched out her arms, and they grasped each other's wrists. "Now pick her up— carefully—and lay her across our arms. Be very careful of that leg. One of you had better walk alongside to support it."

Aretha sobbed quietly as the solemn procession trudged back up the hill and through the deserted streets to the Institute. As they entered the gate, Eleanor said, "We're in for it now."

"I'll take the blame," Susan said. "It was all

my doing."

A strange sight met Miss Read's amazed eyes when she answered the urgent knocking at her door: five snow-covered, red-nosed girls, shivering with cold and fright, carrying two beat-up bread pans and one sobbing girl.

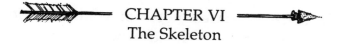

CHAPTER VI
The Skeleton

It was a very subdued Susan who began second-term classes. Not only was Aretha going about on crutches, her leg in a cast, but even worse, Marguerite was lying upstairs very ill. The night of the coasting episode, she had contracted a severe cold. She was susceptible to pneumonia, and Susan was frightened.

"I'm the one who should be struggling around on crutches or lying upstairs sick," she thought miserably, staring unseeing at the open book in front of her. She had been frightened at Miss Read's threat of expulsion and deeply concerned when she was told a letter had been sent home telling how she had broken the rules. Still, the worst seemed to her to be the physical suffering she had caused.

The only consolation she had in those first days of the new term was a letter from Ro that said, "I think I understand, Little Sister, how cooped up you feel in those four walls. But remember that one of the reasons you are at Elizabeth is to learn to fit in. Try to have patience and obey the rules. It would have been a serious blow to Father had you been sent home."

Then Rosalie turned to another subject: "We were all so pleased with your first-term report. Not only were your grades excellent, but your teachers added notes of commendation. They said you have already shown qualities of leadership. That is good for us to hear. Father's whole face brightened when I read him that."

In drawing class, Susan paid no attention to the teacher's explanation of perspective. Her mind was on Rosalie's letter, on Marguerite, and on her own transgressions. She noted, however, that after the teacher turned from the blackboard, the girls started working in their sketch pads. She opened hers and, without thinking what she was doing, began drawing the bones of the leg. Studying the human skeleton in physiology class had stimulated her greatly. She wondered at the bones and how they fit together like an intricate piece of machinery. "How marvelously we're made," she thought as she continued to sketch an entire skeleton. At length she noticed that the teacher was standing beside her.

"That's very good, Susan," she said, "but not what you are supposed to be doing."

Susan's eyes fell in embarrassment.

"Let me have that please," the teacher said. "Now you are to draw the railroad track as I have it on the board, in proper perspective with the rails converging in the distance."

Susan stared at the lines on the blackboard, then went to work.

She was feeling somewhat better the next

day, for Marguerite was showing improvement. In her favorite class, physiology and hygiene, she did a much better job of paying attention than she had done in drawing class the day before.

They had just begun the study of the muscles and their relationship to the bone structure of the body. Miss Higgins explained, "These are the striated muscles. They are composed of long fibers surrounded by a sheath of membrane called the sarcikenna. These muscles are attached to portions of the skeleton by the connective tissue we know as tendons. Contractions of the striated muscles move the bones. That's what makes us able to move an arm." She stretched out her arm as an example.

Susan's hand went up. "But I don't understand what makes them contract."

"A message from the brain, Susan."

Susan frowned. "How does the message get from the brain to our arm or leg?" she asked.

"We will be studying the brain and the nervous system a little later," the teacher replied. "I don't believe we should get into that now."

A few minutes later Susan's hand was up again. Miss Higgins had been explaining a second type of muscle, the smooth muscle.

"If these muscles don't have any sheath around them, what holds them together?" Susan asked.

Miss Higgins looked thoughtfully at her inquiring pupil as she answered her question. At the end of the period, she said, "Susan, will you please stay for a moment?"

"Now what?" Susan wondered. "I suppose I'm asking too many questions."

As she stood by Miss Higgins' side, the teacher took a sheet of drawing paper from her portfolio. Susan saw at once that it contained the skeleton she had been sketching in drawing class.

"This is very good," Miss Higgins said. "And your questions in class, Susan, are intelligent and show a genuine interest. May I ask why your interest in physiology?"

Susan hesitated.

"Perhaps you don't know why?"

Susan found it difficult to reply. She hadn't actually formulated in words, even to herself, what she now found she was trying to say. At last she stammered, "I—I guess it's because—because—well, because I'd like to know how to—to help people when they're hurt or sick."

"I see." Miss Higgins looked more thoughtful than ever as she handed Susan's drawing to her. And Susan herself, as she went to her next class, was so thoughtful that she bumped squarely into another girl.

CHAPTER VII

"To Help My People"

After Marguerite was up and about again, the days raced on quickly for Susan. Before she knew it, the forsythia bushes in the yard were showing yellow and the pussywillows had sprouted soft buds.

"Oh, won't you be glad to get home?" she said to Marguerite. "Sometimes I think I can't wait."

There was still a month before school's end, and in that time startling news came from home. The news came in a letter from Rosalie that brought shouts of disbelief.

"Susette married to that—that Tibbles!" Susan cried. "It just can't be! Why, he's old enough to be her father!"

"And he has children!" Marguerite exclaimed.

Susan nodded. "Two girls. But the worst is, I just don't *like* him!" Even though she had met Thomas Tibbles only once, she had formed an instant dislike for him. She thought him too talkative, too opinionated, and much too egotistical. "And now he's our brother-in-law!" she wailed.

The soft touch of spring was gone, and Susette's marriage was no longer news by the time the girls were back on the reservation.

Being with the family was as wonderful as Susan had dreamed it would be. Riding Pie again, flying across the hills with the wind whipping her braids, was pure joy.

But there was another side to being back on the reservation that caused her distress. The lack of sanitary conditions—of which she had taken no notice before—now appalled her. She talked to Ro about it.

"There's so much sickness on the reservation. I don't think there'd be as much if people were cleaner."

Rosalie was pregnant now, and Susan was enthralled with thoughts of the miracle of birth and of Ro with a baby. But so many babies on the reservation died!

"In our physiology and hygiene class," Susan continued, "we've been learning about bacteria and germs and how they cause disease. They multiply like mad any time, but with heat—they just proliferate."

Ro laughed at Susan's use of the big word, but she listened.

"Ro, there's a lot of cleaning up that needs to be done on this reservation. Dirt and germs go hand in hand." She was thoughtful for a moment, then went on, "I'd like to help improve the health situation, and I think the place to begin is by teaching our people about cleanliness and how to take better care of themselves."

Rosalie nodded.

"Like getting the women to wash their hands before they cook. And washing out wounds and disinfecting them. You know how many times infection sets in from a little cut or scratch. Well, that's why. It's not kept clean, and so germs take over."

Susan did all she could that summer to fit her words to action. In her father's home and in Rosalie's, it was not difficult. But when Susan made suggestions in other homes, she could see resentment, especially in the eyes of the Old Ones.

The summer passed like a gust of wind, and once again Susan and Marguerite were back in their other life, the life of schoolgirls in an elite boarding school.

"I feel like two different people," Susan said soon after their return to Elizabeth. "It's confusing."

But soon they had settled into the school routine. The second year at Elizabeth was less eventful than the first. Susan had learned to curb her impulses, and, instead of landing in mischief, she was devoting herself to leading in scholarship.

Some time after the beginning of the second term, Miss Read called Susan to her office, "I think there is no doubt you will graduate with highest honors," she said.

Susan felt she was expected to say something, so she said, "It will please my father."

Miss Read nodded and asked, "Susan, what do you plan to do when you leave here?"

Susan shook her head. "I don't know."

"Your education mustn't stop here. You have a fine mind. It shouldn't be wasted. What about a career? Would you like to teach?"

"They can always use help at the mission school on the reservation," Susan replied.

"You expect to go back to the reservation?"

"Oh, yes, of course! I want to help my people. I *must help* them only—only—"

"Only you don't know at present how you can best do it. You're young. Don't let this worry you. Just see that your education doesn't end with graduation from Elizabeth."

When graduation time came, Susan still had no idea what lay ahead for her. All she knew was that it would be very good to be home again.

Yet when it came time for good-byes, she found it almost as hard to leave Elizabeth as it had been to leave the reservation.

"I would never have believed," she said to Marguerite when they were on the train, "that I'd be so sad at leaving."

When they arrived home, however, all was excitement and happiness again. There was the thrill of seeing Ro's baby. And their brother Frank was home from Washington on a visit with a friend, Alice Fletcher. Susan saw at once that Miss Fletcher had made a place for herself with both Iron Eye and Rosalie.

"Did Frank explain what Alice Fletcher is doing?" Rosalie asked Susan. "With his help, that is."

"Father told me. He said she was going to write a history of the Omahas."

"Yes," Rosalie said. "She's finding out all she can about the tribe—our history, our customs, our language, our music, everything— and she's going to get it all printed in a book. Isn't that wonderful?"

"I guess," Susan said.

"You *guess*? Don't you see how important it is? Written down, these things will always be kept. If they weren't recorded, they might soon be lost."

Here it was again, Susan thought, this thing called their heritage. It was important to their mother and father, to Susette, and to Rosalie. But why?

Alice Fletcher stayed on through the summer. Each day she rode horseback to find and visit with the Old Ones. At night she wrote in her notebook.

"There must be something wrong with me," Susan thought," that I don't get excited about our past." Perhaps it was because she had come late into the family. Frank and Susette, and even Rosalie, had seen more of the old ways, of the ceremonies and dances and customs. Frank had even gone through the ceremony of becoming a man. Now no such rites were even observed.

It was not until after Grandmother Nicomi took Susan aside one day that summer that she began to understand.

"I want to tell you a story," Nicomi said.

Susan curled up happily at her feet. She loved Nicomi's stories. She loved the soft sound of Grandmother's voice that made her think of water running over stones in the brook.

"It's a story about your mother—whose white name is Mary—at the time when she reached the age for Turning the Child." Nicomi's words took Susan back in time. "It is in the spring, after the first thunder. We have heard the meadow lark's trill."

Susan smiled. The meadow lark's call was to her one of the sweetest sounds of spring. She had missed it sorely in the East.

"It is now the time for the ceremony to make the little ones a part of the tribe. The Sacred Tent is set up and a fire is built in the center. Beside the fire is placed the Sacred Stone. The holy man is within the tent. Many people stand outside. Your mother is a little one of three summers with wide, solemn eyes. I lead her to the tent. No farther can the mother go. I

54

let loose of her hand. I say, 'Go.' I call, 'Venerable One! I desire my child to wear moccasins.'"

"To wear moccasins?" Susan asked, puzzled. "Didn't she have on moccasins?"

"She did. But you do not understand. Let me finish. I say again to the little one who is now your mother, 'Go!' But she only stands with her feet planted wide apart, like a little mule."

Susan laughed.

"So I give her a little push. It makes her run three steps forward, and she is inside the tent. The holy man picks her up. She does not like this, my little one, but she does not cry. The Venerable One chants and faces the child this direction, then that. At last he puts her feet in new moccasins. Then he stands her on the Sacred Stone and cries, 'Ye hills, ye grass, ye creeping things both great and small, I bid you hear! This child has thrown away its baby name. Ho! It goes forth now into the world as Hinnaugonun!'"

Susan had always thought her mother's Indian name, meaning The One Woman, was lovely. But never before had she heard the story of her receiving it.

"So now Hinnaugonun runs from the tent to me, pointing to her new moccasins, very proud," said Nicomi. "But I am even more proud. My child is now an Omaha."

Susan sat very still when the story was ended. Why had it affected her so deeply? It must have been the importance given to the child's becoming a member of the tribe that had touched her. It was also the ceremony. In her mind, she had seen the tent, the congregation of her people, and the small child starting out on the big adventure that was life. New moccasins.

Yes, there were things in the old ways that were poetic and lovely. She was glad Alice Fletcher and Frank were writing them down. She knew that her father was glad too. For the first time she realized that he loved the old ways as much as anyone. But he saw that, in order to survive in a world where the white men were many and the red men few, the Indian must adopt new ways.

PHOTOGRAPHS
Family, Friends & Walthill

Medical College of Pennsylvania/Nebraska State Historical Society
Dr. Susan La Flesche Picotte

Nebraska State Historical Society

Nicomi [Nekomi], Susan's Grandmother

Nebraska State Historical Society

Mary Gale La Flesche, Susan's Mother

Nebraska State Historical Society
Joseph La Flesche, Susan's Father

Nebraska State Historical Society

Susette La Flesche, Susan's Sister

Nebraska State Historical Society

Rosalie La Flesche, Susan's Sister

Nebraska State Historical Society

Marguerite La Flesche, Susan's Sister

Nebraska State Historical Society

Dr. Susan La Flesche Picotte, later life

Nebraska State Historical Society

Nettie Fremont (?), Mary Tyndall, Susan La Flesche,
Marguerite La Flesche, approximately 1880

Nebraska State Historical Society

Francis [Frank] La Flesche, Susan's Brother

Nebraska State Historical Society

Alice Fletcher

Nebraska State Historical Society

Walthill Hospital built by Dr. Susan La Flesche Picotte
This facility now houses the Dr. Susan La Flesche Picotte Center.

Nebraska State Historical Society

Dr. Susan La Flesche Picotte's home in Walthill

CHAPTER VIII

A Friend in Alice Fletcher

Very soon Susan saw why Rosalie was pleased to have Alice Fletcher with them. Although Susan and Marguerite spent their days assisting at the mission school and Alice spent her days gleaning information about the tribe, all three often spent the evening at Rosalie's.

One evening Susan was telling how Marguerite had won over a stubborn little boy whom the teachers had been unable to teach a word of English. "She's so good with children, I think she's a natural-born teacher," she ended.

Alice Fletcher was listening with interest. Then she said, "And you, Susan? Are you good with children?"

"Not particularly," Susan replied. "I just grab them and say, 'Come with me and wash your hands.'"

"Marguerite, do you plan to be a teacher?" Alice asked.

"I guess, if they want me." Then she looked at Rosalie, nursing her baby. "But I want to get married too."

Rosalie smiled at her, and Alice nodded. Then she turned to Susan. "And do you too plan to teach and get married?"

Susan sighed. "I don't know," she said.

Some weeks later, summer had settled on the reservation. The hot sun had curled the corn in the field and had caused the dogs, with their tongues lolling, to hunt for a patch of shade. Again the four young women sat on Rosalie's porch one evening searching for a wisp of breeze.

"I've been thinking about you girls," Alice Fletcher said to Susan and Marguerite. "You really should have more education if you're going to teach."

Susan's thoughts drifted away, and she remembered Miss Read's admonition that she must continue her education. But how? Right now it was so hot, and she felt so lazy that she didn't really care to pursue the thought.

Then suddenly she heard what Alice was saying, and her indifference vanished. "Hampton?" she questioned.

"Yes, it's a normal school and agricultural institute in Hampton, Virginia."

"Virginia?" Rosalie exclaimed. "Would it be near Washington, D. C.?"

"It isn't far," Alice replied. "It's a school that was first established for Negro youths, but now they are admitting Indians also. I think it would be well to send in your records from Elizabeth and make application for you to enter."

"Oh, Alice, that would be wonderful!" Rosalie exclaimed. "And the girls would be near you and Frank."

"Of course the school may be filled for this fall."

Susan said nothing. A school where they taught you to teach? She didn't really want to teach, but she supposed it would be a logical way to help her people.

Then something Alice had said registered with her, and she asked, "Normal school and agricultural school? You mean girls learn to farm?"

Alice Fletcher smiled. "No, I think it's the boys who take the agricultural courses."

"Boys?" Marguerite and Susan chorused.

"Yes, it's a coeducational school."

This was a new and startling concept to the three sisters sitting on the step.

"Boys and girls go to the same school?!" Susan asked in disbelief.

"Oh, yes. There are many coeducational schools and colleges in the country. Shall we write a letter to Hampton tomorrow, Rosalie?"

Rosalie hesitated, and Susan was sure she knew why. Finally Ro said, "We'd better talk to Father first."

"Of course," Alice agreed.

Susan knew that, though her father was eager for his children to become well educated, he still held to the tribal idea that young men and young women did not mingle socially. What would his reaction be to Alice Fletcher's suggestion that his daughters attend a school where they would mix freely with young men?

She did not have long to wait for his reaction to the Hampton proposal. Believing that time was important, Alice Fletcher went the following day to talk to Iron Eye.

"I should like to put in an application for Susan and Marguerite to enter a school near Washington this fall," she said.

Iron Eye looked pleased. He nodded in approval.

"It is the Hampton Normal and Agricultural Institute. It trains young women to be teachers and young men to be farmers."

Instantly Iron Eye's brows came together. "It is two schools?" he asked.

"No, it is all one school, with different courses offered in the two programs," Alice Fletcher explained.

"One school altogether? Boys and girls together at this school?"

"Yes, Mr. La Flesche," Alice Fletcher said patiently. "This is a very common practice."

"It is not good. No!" Iron Eye's face had gone stern. "My girls will not go to this school."

Alice stood up. "You think about it," she said pleasantly.

Several days went by with no mention of Hampton. Then one evening, Alice Fletcher said with a little twinkle in her eye, "Do you feel like writing a letter, Rosalie?"

"You mean..." Susan cried.

"Yes, your father has agreed to let you go."

"What changed his mind?" asked Marguerite.

"The fact that he so much wants you girls to continue your education. We will have to ask for scholarships, of course. If you declare your intention to come back to the reservation to teach, I think you'll stand a fair chance of getting them."

For Marguerite this was easy, but for Susan it posed problems. "What if I *don't* come back here to teach?" she asked.

"Right now doesn't it look as if you will?" Alice asked reasonably.

"I suppose so," Susan said. She saw Rosalie eyeing her speculatively. "She knows teaching isn't what I want," she thought. "At any rate, Hampton would mean additional education. I guess I'd better declare my intentions!"

Alice Fletcher wasted no time. She and Rosalie had the applications ready to go the next day. Then began the time of waiting.

Never too long on patience, Susan became more and more restless as July ended and the August days dragged by, swept by a searing wind that helped no one's disposition.

"I just don't think we're going to get in," she said one day to Marguerite.

"I don't either, so I think I'd better apply for a teaching job at the mission for this fall," Marguerite replied. "Are you going to, too?"

Susan shook her head. "I don't think so. I don't know what I'll do if we aren't admitted. I've got to go to school somewhere."

But where? And how? These questions haunted her as time went by, and still they did not hear from Hampton. She and Marguerite would not be able to go anywhere unless they had scholarships, and scholarships had to be funded. That was the whole problem, she thought angrily. Money was too scarce to do more than feed the family and take care of their daily needs. There was none left over for schooling.

But then there came a day in late August when Alice Fletcher came riding in from town waving a letter.

"Ro! Marg! Sue!" she called. "There's a letter from Hampton!"

They all came running. Rosalie opened the letter, and Susan knew by her face: They were going to Hampton!

CHAPTER IX

Hampton–And Boys!

"It's just about as different from Elizabeth as summer from winter!" Susan commented after she and Marguerite had been deposited in Winona Hall at Hampton by their brother and Alice Fletcher.

Hampton Normal and Agricultural Institute was, indeed, a totally different world from the Omaha Reservation in Nebraska and from the protected, sheltered life at Elizabeth Institute. As students began to arrive, Susan was shocked to see as many blacks as Indians, for she had seen few black people in her life. It was also a shock to see young men everywhere she looked. She could walk on the campus, alone if she wished, without having to ask permission and without a chaperone. People spoke to her, both Indians and Negroes, both young men and young women.

On Friday evening the housemother called a meeting of Winona Hall girls. "I wanted to explain," she said, "that on one Saturday evening a month the boys are allowed to come to supper and to stay afterward for an hour of games with you girls."

An audible gasp arose.

"This will be a time for learning some of the etiquette involved in social situations where both young men and young women are present. Our first sociable will be tomorrow evening."

"Games?" Susan exclaimed in bewilderment after the meeting. Of course she and her sisters had played games as children: Fox and Goose when there was new snow, and Hide-and-Seek during long summer evenings. But now when they were grown up, were they still going to play games? And with young men?

By Saturday evening, Winona Hall had reached a high pitch of excitement. Susan and Marguerite were as excited as anyone there. When supper was over, all the students assembled in the parlor, girls on one side of the room, boys on the other. Susan's heart was fluttering. How would her first sociable go?

Then she forgot about herself, for, looking across the room, she saw how frightened and forlorn many of the young men looked. Some wouldn't raise their eyes from the floor. Her own eyes roved the length of the row of boys sitting uneasily in the straight chairs along the wall. Directly across from her was a young man whom she thought the handsomest Indian she had ever seen. But he was obviously most unhappy. If he would just look up, she would smile at him.

Finally, when the General (as everyone called General Armstrong who headed the school) had called for attention, the young man's eyes came up, and Susan flashed her smile. But his eyes were on the General, and it was the young man seated next to him who caught Susan's smile and sent her one in return. Now it was time for her own eyes to fall. "*He's* not shy or unhappy," she thought. "He's probably been here before."

The General first explained a game called Rain a Little. Then he said, "Now if about six of you young men would each choose a lady partner and come out into the middle of the floor, please."

Quick as a flash of lightning, the young man who had smiled at Susan was at her side. "Will you be my partner?" he asked.

Susan stood up. She saw that Marguerite too had been chosen.

"First," said the General, "we will learn about making introductions."

So it was that Susan learned her partner's name was Ashley. It was all very exciting, but she found herself thinking, "I'd much rather be meeting the handsome, sad-eyed one."

Every time there was a boy-choose-girl game, Ashley made a dash for Susan. And when the General blew his whistle and called the Grand March, it was the same. Again she noticed that Marguerite was one of the first chosen. But as the line formed, a number of students remained seated.

"Come now," urged the General. "Everybody in the Grand March! You boys just take the girl nearest to you." He crossed to where the sad-eyed young man sat unmoving. "Here, Ikinicapi," he said, half lifting the handsome young man from the chair, "you take Eliza."

So, his name was Ikinicapi.

CHAPTER X

Ikinicapi

"Ashley likes Susan! Ashley likes Susan!" The chant followed Susan and Marguerite as they climbed the stairs after their memorable first Saturday night at Hampton.

Susan looked over her shoulder and laughed. "So maybe he does," she said. She felt flushed and elated. She would have to agree with Marguerite that a coeducational school had advantages. She'd had no idea that being singled out by a young man would be so stimulating.

When they reached their room, she asked Marguerite, who seemed unusually quiet, "Did you meet anyone you liked?"

"Oh, yes," Marguerite said. "The one I marched with. His name is Charles Picotte."

As the weeks went by, Marguerite and Charles were frequently together. But with Susan it was different. Although Ashley was always appearing after church to walk home with her or demanding her for his partner in Saturday night games, there were other young men who also sought her attention, and she made it clear to Ashley that he was not the only one.

"I like a lot of the boys," she explained to Marguerite. "I don't like Ashley any better than the others. It's different with you and Charlie, isn't it?"

"I guess it is," Marguerite agreed. "He's so nice, Sue. I do like him ever so much."

"Well, I have to quit thinking about boys and get my algebra done," Susan said.

Already Susan was leading her classes at Hampton, and other students were asking her to help them. But there was someone she wished she could help...someone who did not ask for help. She said as much to Marguerite.

"Who's that?" Marguerite asked.

"Ikinicapi."

"Why Ikinicapi?"

"Oh, he doesn't handle the English language well at all, and I know he's having trouble. He looks so unhappy. Isn't he the handsomest thing, Marg?"

"Hmmm," Marguerite said, looking at her sister speculatively. "Maybe Sue likes T. I."

"T. I.?"

"That's what Charlie calls him. It's short for Thomas Ikinicapi."

"He's Dakota Sioux, you know." Susan was thinking how the Dakota Sioux and the Omahas had long been enemies. "I wonder why they're our enemy," she said aloud.

"Because in the old days they were always chasing us. They wanted all the good hunting grounds."

"But that shouldn't matter now."

"No, but don't forget that Father's partner, Logan Fontanelle, was killed by Sioux, and not so long ago."

Susan sighed and let the subject drop.

She found that, whatever she was doing, thoughts of Ikinicapi kept creeping in. He had never asked to walk with her, had never chosen her for a partner at sociables. Yet occasionally in the chapel or in the dining room, she would feel his eyes on her; but when she looked his way, he would look toward the floor.

She learned that Ikinicapi was a member of a group called the Helping Hand Society and that they had undertaken a project that pleased her greatly. Suddenly she felt a need to talk to Rosalie. She sat down at her desk and began to write.

> Dear Ro,
>
> It's so good of you to write us all the time and tell us about what's going on at home. There's something happening here that I want to tell you about. There's a club called the Helping Hand Society, made up largely of Sioux, and you'd never guess who they're helping right now: an *Omaha* family! Isn't that wonderful?

Marguerite came into the room while Susan was writing. "Sue, aren't you supposed to be on duty in the dairy this afternoon?"

"Oh, yes. I'm glad you reminded me." She picked up her writing materials and ran down to the dairy.

The Hampton setup included a work program through which every student was given experience in various departments of the school. The program did double duty: it taught the students skills, and it reduced the cost of labor required to operate the school.

Susan had already learned to make butter, and, as she hurried along the corridor to the dairy, she was thinking that, if the butter would just set up for her in good time this afternoon, she could finish her letter to Rosalie. But when she entered the sunny room with its sweet-sour smell of milk and sour cream and cheese, she came to a sudden halt, for beside the cheese vat stood Ikinicapi.

"Hello," she said. "I didn't know you'd be here."

He looked at her and smiled, and for an instant her heart seemed to stop. Then he went on about his work, and she turned to hers.

After a little while she said, "You're in the Helping Hands, aren't you?"

He nodded.

"I think it's wonderful that you're helping the Omaha family that lost their home in a tornado."

He beamed at her. "We collect money," he said.

"I know," Susan replied. "I heard you'd gone to the merchants in town."

"Merchants?" he asked, looking puzzled.

"The—the stores," Susan explained.

Ikinicapi nodded vigorously. "Much money," he said.

"So the Dakota Sioux are no longer our enemy?" she asked.

She did not know how well he understood, for he pondered a moment before he answered. But when he spoke, he said, looking directly at her, "Enemy, no. Friend."

This time Susan's eyes fell, for she was sure he meant the remark personally.

It was evening before she got back to finish Ro's letter:

> I had to quit and go to work in the dairy, but I'd started to tell you the Helping Hands are collecting money for the Omaha family that lost their house in the tornado. There's a fellow in the society named Ikinicapi who was telling me about it. Ro, he's the handsomest Indian I've ever seen. He's only smiled at me a couple of times, but I think he likes me.
>
> We were sorry to hear about Alice Fletcher's riding accident. Were any bones broken? Do write and tell us how she is getting along.
>
> Well, I'd better get to studying. Tell

Mother and Father we are doing fine.
We have plenty to eat, and we are
studying hard. Kiss your precious
little Maidie for me, and tell Ed I said
hello.

Your loving, loving,
Sue

The following Sunday morning Susan stood
impatiently at the door waiting for Marguerite,
to go to church. As they were sitting down,
Susan felt compelled to look behind her. "It was
as if a magnet was drawing me," she told her
sister later. "I knew I shouldn't look around,
but I couldn't help myself." The magnet was
Ikinicapi who was sitting directly behind.

When the services were over, Charles
Picotte was waiting for Marguerite, and at his
side was Thomas Ikinicapi. T. I. didn't say a
word. He just fell in beside Susan, and the four
of them started toward Winona. To her
amazement, Susan could think of nothing to
say.

"It's—it's a nice day, isn't it?" she managed
finally.

The young man at her side nodded his head
and gave her a radiant smile. "Nice," he agreed.
"Nice," he repeated enthusiastically.

"Oh," Susan thought, "I'm so glad to see
him looking happy. He usually looks so sad and
lonely." She smiled at him.

As they neared the steps of Winona Hall, they saw Miss Patterson, who was one of Susan's favorite teachers. Miss Patterson was just opening the door. She recognized the couples approaching, and Susan saw the look of surprise on her face, followed by an unmistakable look of disapproval.

"Now why did she look at us like that?" Susan wondered.

CHAPTER XI
To Be A Doctor

Susan did not have long to wonder about Miss Patterson's disapproving look. Following the next Saturday evening sociable—at which Thomas Ikinicapi chose Susan for every game and beat Ashley to her side for the Grand March—Miss Patterson called her in.

"Susan, I wonder if you've thought about the effect of your encouraging Thomas Ikinicapi," she said.

Susan almost jumped. "Why, Miss Patterson, I haven't made the advances. He has."

"That may be," the teacher said, "but you are encouraging him, every time you let him walk you home or take you as a partner. It's not that he isn't a nice young man. It's just that—well, you are far superior to him intellectually, Susan."

"But I think I can help him with his studies," Susan said. "He's trying. And, if I'm beyond him, it's because I've had advantages he hasn't had. That's not his fault."

"I'm not blaming him for not doing well in his studies, Susan. You are missing the point of what I am saying."

Susan didn't think she was missing the point. Miss Patterson disapproved of her going with T. I. because she felt Susan was too good for him. Sue resented this fiercely, but she said no more.

"Just think about it, Susan," Miss Patterson said. "You are headed for great things, and you don't want to get into an entanglement that would ruin your future."

As the winter slipped into spring Susan continued to see Thomas Ikinicapi. Miss Patterson was not the only one who disapproved of the couple or the only one who spoke to Susan about it. But, however much time and thought Susan devoted to T. I., her grades remained exemplary.

"They can't say I'm neglecting my studies," she said to herself as she walked out of one end-of-term examination in which she was sure she had answered every question correctly.

T. I. was waiting for her. "Let's take walk," he said.

"Let's take *a* walk," she corrected him.

T. I. shrugged, and they strolled in the sun, the scent of lilacs reaching them on the soft spring breeze.

"Nice day!" T. I. said, and he put so much into the two words that Susan laughed aloud.

"Why do you laugh?" he wanted to know.

"Oh, because I agree with you. It's such a lovely day! Spring does something to you, doesn't it? It makes you so—so sensitive and vulnerable."

She knew he wouldn't understand the meaning of "vulnerable," but perhaps it was better that he didn't. Eager as she was to get home and see her family and to roam the wooded hills, it was not going to be easy to say good-bye to T. I.—to think of a whole summer without him.

"I'll write you every week," she promised.

"I do not write so good," he said sadly, shaking his head.

"You write to me anyway," Susan said. "Don't use that as an excuse."

Back home again on the reservation, however, she became busy nursing Alice Fletcher, and it was not until she saw an envelope addressed to her in T. I.'s nearly illegible hand that she realized she had not kept her promise.

She was at Rosalie's when the letter was handed to her. "Oh, dear!" she said, suddenly feeling very guilty. "It's from T. I., and I haven't written him."

She saw that Rosalie was watching her thoughtfully as she tore open the envelope and scanned the penciled lines. It didn't take long to read. "Well, he's happy to be home. I'm glad," she said. That was about all he'd had to say except that he was thinking of her. It was a poor letter, but at least he had done better than she had.

"You're quite fond of T. I., Sue?" Rosalie said.

"Yes," Susan replied. "He's a very dear boy—so gentle and good—and the handsomest thing you ever saw. I wish you could meet him, Ro."

She stuffed the letter in her pocket. "I must get back to my patient," she said.

Susan had been appalled when she first reached home, both to discover that Alice Fletcher was very ill and that Rosalie, whose hands were already filled with her growing family, was taking care of her.

"What happened?" she asked Rosalie. "You wrote about Alice being thrown by a skittish horse, and you said her leg had been injured. But I thought you said she was getting along all right."

"She was," Rosalie replied. "Then this young doctor she was going to started her on leg exercises, and her leg began hurting. Pretty soon she had pain in her other leg too and in her arms and back, and they decided she had rheumatic fever."

"She has fever all right," Susan said. "Well, you're through nursing her, wearing yourself out, Rosalie Farley. You look exhausted. I'm taking over here and now."

Susan had done just that. With T. I.'s letter in her pocket, she brought a basin of water and started bathing her patient. Her thoughts again had turned to T. I. and how often he was sick. Marguerite too. Why? Something must have happened when they were children to damage some organ of the body or to impair its function. She wished she knew more about such things. How important doctors were! If only they could tell people what to do to keep from getting sick instead of how to get well afterward, they would be even more important.

That night she wrote T. I. She thanked him for his letter and told him what she was doing and why she hadn't written. She sat for a long time over the letter, yet it was nearly as short as his. "I certainly didn't have much to say," she thought as she sealed the envelope.

She continued to receive his short letters, one every week, as the hot summer dragged on. She answered each one, telling him how the hot winds were stirring up dust clouds, how her patient was slowly improving, and how good it was to be with her family.

One afternoon after Alice Fletcher was able to sit up, and Susan and Rosalie were keeping her company, the conversation turned to Alice's work. "I know I shouldn't be impatient," she said, "but there's still so much I want to do before I have to go back to Washington."

"It's a wonderful thing you're doing for us," Susan said. "Getting down all the tribal ceremonies and songs and everything." To herself she said, "How my attitude has changed!"

"I still lack a great deal," Alice sighed. "It takes so long, hunting up the Old Ones, finding the ones who performed the rites, and then getting them to tell me about them. Some of them are very reluctant."

"I was thinking," said Rosalie, "that maybe we could get some of them to come to you."

Alice shook her head.

"They'd come to Father's house. And I think most of them would talk if he asked them to," Rosalie continued.

"Of course they would!" Susan agreed. "Father realizes the importance of what you're doing. He'd see that they cooperated."

"Your father is very forceful," Alice Fletcher agreed. "And do you know, Susan, you take after him. You're like him in many ways, your forcefulness and firmness among them."
"I am?" Susan asked.

Rosalie and Alice smiled at each other.

"You are indeed," Alice said. They were all quiet for a moment, then she went on. "I'm sure you've given thought to how you are going to use your ability, Sue. It mustn't go to waste, you know."

"It won't," Susan replied promptly. Had Rosalie said something to Alice Fletcher? Everyone seemed to be afraid Susan would marry Ikinicapi and waste her talents. Even so, her desire to help her people never wavered.

79

"I'm glad to hear you say that." Susan realized that Alice Fletcher was responding to her last remark, but it was as if Alice spoke from a great distance. "You look very thoughtful, Susan," the patient added.

"I was thinking that in three more weeks we go back to school."

"And you will be glad to go?"

"Yes, in a way. I'll be glad to get back to my studies and..."

"And to that handsomest of all Indians named Ikinicapi?" Alice Fletcher teased.

"Yes," Susan said slowly, "I'll be glad to see him. But I will hate to leave you before you are entirely well."

"You are a conscientious and lovely child," Alice Fletcher said. Then she corrected herself, "Except that you're not a child. You are a woman."

Susan thought, "And a woman with some difficult decisions to make."

She made one of those decisions before she left for Hampton.

Alice Fletcher had felt well enough one afternoon to go to Iron Eye's house for an interview with an old medicine man of the tribe. Susan had taken notes for her so that her task would be less arduous. Now the Old One had gone, and Rosalie, Ed, and the children had come to have supper with the family.

"I have something I want to say to you

while we're all together," Susan said. There was something in her voice that demanded the attention of all of them, even the two children playing on the floor. All eyes were turned on her. "It's something I've been thinking about for a long time, and I've finally come to a decision. Taking care of Alice this summer helped. The human body interests me more than anything else. When something goes wrong with it, I want to know how to fix it."

There was a happy smile on Rosalie's face. "You're going to be a nurse," she said.

"No." Susan said. "If it is humanly possible, I am going to become a doctor."

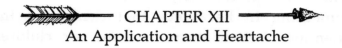
An Application and Heartache

The announcement Susan made to her family had been almost as startling to her as to the others. How was she to become a doctor? Whoever heard of an Indian doctor, and a woman at that?

"There are some fine women doctors," Alice Fletcher said quietly, almost as if she had heard Susan's thoughts, "and you will add to their ranks."

No one spoke for several minutes after Alice's encouraging remark.

"They're stunned," Susan thought. Then she looked at Rosalie, and the proud glow in her eyes was enough. Susan needed no words from her. She looked at her mother. Mother's face was impassive as always, and, as always, she remained silent. Then Susan's eyes turned to her father. Slowly he stood up and straightened to his full height. He extended his hand to her, and when she took it his strong fingers pressed till it hurt.

"Proud," he said. "We are very proud."

All of this was well and good. She had taken her stand. But how to implement it was another matter. "I have a year," she thought. "A year before graduation from Hampton, a year to find out if I can get into a medical school and obtain financing."

"There's a women's medical college in Philadelphia," Alice told her before she and Marguerite left for Hampton. "Why don't you investigate it?"

Having the name of a college and knowing where it was located made her idea seem more real and more possible. She was glad she had kept her grades up. Alice said medical colleges had very high standards for admission.

"What are you going to do about T. I.?" Marguerite asked her when they were alone.

"I don't know," Susan said. "I honestly don't know, Marg."

The problem of T. I. loomed larger when they were back on campus. On the reservation when her only contact with him had been through his brief notes, she had been able to admit to herself that perhaps there was something in what Miss Patterson and the others said. But when they were back together again, it was another matter. Her mind might be able to see that such a union would not do, but her heart denied it strenuously.

"I miss you so bad," T. I. said the first time they were alone together. "I thought summer would never stop."

"End," Susan said automatically. But her voice held none of the austerity of criticism. Only gentleness and love.

"End," T. I. repeated, turning a smile on her

that constricted her heart and brought tears very close.

She had not told him of her decision. "I guess I'm being a coward," she thought. But those first weeks of renewed companionship were so beautiful that she could not bear to spoil them.

To Miss Patterson and to General Armstrong, however, she revealed her plan, for she would need their help.

"This is wonderful news! Wonderful!" the General exclaimed. "It will be the best thing that's happened yet at Hampton."

Susan knew this was high praise, because Hampton Institute, which had opened shortly after the Civil War, had been in operation nearly twenty years.

"But—but how do I apply?" she asked.

"We will write a letter to the Woman's Medical College* of Pennsylvania immediately," he promised. "They will inform us."

Sunday night came, and as usual T. I. was waiting to walk her home after church. He did not, however, smile at her as usual, and she knew at once that something was wrong. She tried teasing him about his sad face, hoping to change his mood. But he walked at her side in solemn silence.

At length she said, "What is it, T. I.? What's wrong?"

[*Previously called the Women's Medical College in other editions]

"You are going to be a doctor?" he said then.

Susan caught her breath. Oh, no! How had he heard? She thought no one knew but Miss Patterson and General Armstrong—and Marguerite, of course. Marg must have told Charlie, and Charlie had told T. I. For a moment she was angry with Marguerite. Then she thought, "No, it's my own fault. Marguerite didn't know I hadn't told T. I.—and I *should* have told him!"

"Oh, T. I.!" she cried. "I'm so sorry. I'd meant to tell you only—only..."

"Is it true?"

"Yes, it's true that I'm going to try, T. I. I'm going to apply for entrance to medical college next year. But of course I don't know if I'll be accepted."

"You will get in," T. I. said. There was a deep, resigned sadness in his voice that hurt her deeply.

"I'm sorry," she said again, her voice breaking.

"Do not be sorry," T. I. said. "You will make a fine doctor."

Susan climbed the stairs to her room slowly. She knew T. I. was accepting this as final. But did it have to be the end of their relationship? Wasn't there some other way?

When she opened the door to her room, she saw that Marguerite was there before her. Deep in her own thoughts and her own unhappiness,

Susan did not notice that her sister's face was glowing.

Marguerite's voice was soft. "When you've hung up your coat, come here. I have something to show you."

Susan complied, walking like a zombie to her sister's side.

Marguerite held out her left hand. On her fourth finger was a silver ring. "He made it for me himself," she said.

"Oh, Marg, darling! You mean you're engaged?" Susan threw her arms around her sister and hugged her tight. But Sue kept her face turned away. There was a big lump in her throat, and she bit her lip hard for control.

"Yes. We're going to be married as soon as we finish school."

"Oh, Marg, that's wonderful. I'm so happy for you."

"We thought we'd see if we could have a party to announce it."

"Of course. We'll have a splendid party!"

"Sue, we wondered—you and T. I.?"

Susan knew what she meant: Would she and T. I. also want to announce their engagement? She turned her back and stood looking out the window into the darkness. She found she could not speak. She shook her head.

"I'm sorry. I'm sorry I asked, Sue." Marguerite's arms were around her. Her sympathy was too much. Susan burst into tears.

CHAPTER XIII

Accepted For Medical School

Marguerite's engagement to Charlie was announced, and at the party many eyes were turned inquiringly on Susan and T. I. He had said no more about Susan's plans, nor had Susan brought up the subject. Outwardly their relationship remained the same, but there was a hopeless expression in T. I.'s eyes that wrung Susan's heart. "What can I say to him?" she wondered.

One night she tried to explain. "It's so important in our family that we help our tribe. Father's whole life has been devoted to trying to get the Omahas to understand that it's a white man's world now and that our people must adapt."

T. I.'s silence defeated her, and she gave up.

Another time she mentioned Susette and all she was doing. "So you see, it's—well, it's expected of us."

This time he surprised her. "Marg and Charlie, they will marry. She will teach," he said.

Susan nodded.

"And your sister Rosalie. She married and stayed on the reservation."

How could she explain that their own situation was different? There seemed to be no way to keep from hurting him further. No, there was no way to make him understand. Or perhaps he did understand, and the hopelessness of his knowledge made him determined to deny it.

She felt a deep sadness, but on the surface things seemed to go well with her. The senior class elected her their president.

"I don't know what I can do for the class," she said to Marguerite, "but I'll try."

Marguerite laughed. "You always say that: 'I'll try.' Did you know it's become your trademark?"

Susan shook her head. "I guess it's true I'm willing to tackle almost anything," she said after a moment's thought, "at least if I think I can do any good."

One day General Armstrong called her in. "I have heard from the Woman's Medical College in Philadelphia," he said. "They have sent this form for you to fill out. Also you are to write a letter telling why you wish to become a doctor. We will take care of the rest. They want a transcript of your record from Elizabeth Institute."

"I can get that," Susan began.

But the General interrupted. "No need, m'dear. We've already written. They also want a transcript of your grades here and letters of recommendation from your teachers and from me. You can ask your teachers to write them for you. I've already drafted my letter, and I'll tell you, Susan, that it contains the highest recommendation I have ever written for one of our students."

"Thank you, sir."

She walked out of the General's office holding the form carefully, but not yet reading it. She was elated, of course, to be taking the first step toward her goal. But she was more than a little frightened. What if they didn't accept her? Or, if they did, what if she couldn't understand the subjects? What if she should fail? Was this too big a thing she had set out to do? Too big for an Indian? Too big for Susan La Flesche?

"Well, all I can do is try," she thought. Then she laughed, remembering what Marguerite had told her.

Susan filled out the application carefully. Then she turned to the more difficult task of writing the letter to accompany it. She chewed on the end of her pen for a long time. How could she put into words the burning desire to help her people that had colored every day of her life? How could anyone in Philadelphia be made to understand the physical suffering on the Omaha Reservation in Nebraska?

They were well into the second term when she received a summons to come to General Armstrong's office. She could feel her pulse pounding in her ears as she hurried to respond.

He had heard from Philadelphia!? What if she hadn't been accepted? And, if she had, what then? She would have to come to some decision about T. I.

"Come in, Susan," the General said. "Have that chair."

She sat down, grateful for the opportunity. Her legs were as weak as a newborn calf's.

"I've been doing a bit of figuring. At present," General Armstrong went on, "you stand second highest in your class. Unless the picture should change radically as a result of second-term examinations, which seems most unlikely, you will be salutatorian."

Susan gulped. The general's words had nothing to do with hearing from the medical school. This was so completely alien to what she had expected that she found it difficult to absorb.

"Yes," the General nodded. "Salutatorian. This means you will give an address at commencement, and I thought you might like to be considering a topic."

It was an honor to be salutatorian, and Susan knew her family would be proud. Perhaps it would even be a bonus toward admission to medical school. How long was it going to take them to make up their minds about that? She didn't think she could bear the waiting much longer.

But spring came, and still she had not heard.

"Have you decided on a topic for your speech?" Marguerite asked her one night.

"More or less. But I haven't turned it in. I thought I'd speak on my childhood and womanhood."

Marguerite laughed. "You haven't had much of your womanhood yet, Sue."

"Oh, you don't understand. I'm going to talk about my past and my future."

"How do you know what your future's going to be?"

"I don't. Not really. I suppose that part will be more like a dream."

"Well, my future is no dream. They've just told me I'll have to come back next fall in order to have enough credits to graduate."

"Really, Marg?" Susan's eyes were full of sympathy. "You've missed so much, being sick." Then she thought about her sister's plans to marry. "What about you and Charlie?" she asked.

"Charlie will be coming back too."

"Oh, I'm glad. That will make it better for you."

"Only we can't get married as soon as we'd planned."

"But you'll be together."

The note of sadness in Susan's voice came through clearly to her sister. It said plainly: "And T. I. and I will *not* be together."

So Susan had the topic for her address, and

91

she knew in general what she wanted to say. "But what am I going to wear?" she thought ruefully.

When she broached this problem to Marguerite, her sister said, "Somehow we'll have to get material for a new dress for you. I'll help you make it."

"But first we must have money to buy material," Susan laughed. Getting the money seemed as unlikely as a walk on the moon.

Several weeks later, however, when they received a letter from Rosalie, there was a dollar bill enclosed. "We are so proud of our Sue," she wrote. "We want her to have a lovely new dress for commencement. I hope you can get some pretty material for this dollar. It's from Nicomi."

"From Nicomi?" Sue cried, tears in her eyes. "Bless her. Bless our dear old grandmother. She remembers that a woman wants to look pretty—as pretty as she can, that is."

The dress was made, and the speech was written, both with care. It was only a week until graduation, and Susan still had not heard from the medical school.

"Do you think my not hearing means I wasn't accepted?" she asked Miss Patterson.

"I doubt it. I think they would surely let you know one way or the other."

"Do you honestly think I stand a chance?" she asked, looking straight into Miss Patterson's eyes.

"Your grades are excellent, and I know you received the highest of recommendations. I don't see why not."

"I'm an Indian, Miss Patterson." It was the thing Susan kept thinking about, the thing she feared would bar her.

"I surely hope that would make no difference to the admissions board," Miss Patterson replied indignantly.

Susan said no more, but she was not convinced.

With only three days left at Hampton, a letter finally came addressed to Miss Susan La Flesche...a letter that was not in Rosalie's or their brother Frank's or Alice Fletcher's handwriting. Susan held the long envelope unopened. "Oh, Marg," she said in a very small voice, "this is it, and I'm scared to open it."

"Here, let me," Marguerite said, taking the letter form her. She tore the envelope open neatly and pulled out the letter. "There. But you read it." She stood back and waited as Susan unfolded the single sheet.

In an instant Susan threw the letter into the air and caught her sister around the waist. "They accepted me! They accepted me!" she shrieked. She twirled Marguerite in a wild dance of triumph. "They took me, Marg! They took me—an Indian!"

Susan took her letter to Miss Patterson.

"That's wonderful, dear," the teacher said. "We're proud of you. Have you told anyone else?"

"Only Marguerite."

"I think you should take your letter to General Armstrong. He'll want to announce the good news at commencement." So Susan took her good news to the General.

On the night before the big day, Susan decided she was as ready as she would ever be. There was just one thing that remained to be done—the hardest thing of all. She must tell T. I.

After supper she and Marguerite went for a walk. They knew Charlie and T. I. would join them. This had become a pattern. Two by two they had taken many walks together during the soft spring evenings.

"I have to tell T. I. tonight," she said, biting her lip.

Marguerite nodded. "Charlie and I will leave you alone."

For a few minutes after Marguerite and Charlie had left them, Susan walked silently at T. I.'s side.

"I have something to tell you, T. I.," she finally managed, feeling physically ill from the effort. She couldn't go on.

T. I. reached for her hand. "I know," he said. "You got into the doctor school. Don't be sad."

"Oh, T. I.!" She was so grateful to him for helping her. But how could she not be sad? She could barely speak. "Not sad? I—I don't think I can bear it, T. I."

"You will be all right."

She shook her head. "Maybe—maybe I won't make it in medical school."

"Not make the grades? Of course you will."

They had come to a bench beside the path, and with one accord they sat down. Susan was fighting for control. "What—what will you do next year?"

"Come back to Hampton. My grades are not good like Sue's."

The thought of T. I. here next year, alone, and of herself alone in Philadelphia was too much. She could no longer hold back the tears.

T. I. took her chin in his hand. "No tears, little Sue. Don't be sad. Tomorrow is your big day. I am so proud."

Susan wakened very early the next morning. She lay listening to the little predawn sounds: the twittering of the birds, the stirring of a breeze, the distant crowing of a rooster. Her first thoughts were of T. I.

Then she turned her mind to the day before

her. She recited her speech from beginning to end. "I didn't miss a word," she thought. "But standing on the platform with the General and the teachers behind me and people filling the seats out front—that may make a difference." She had the speech written out, and she comforted herself with the thought that if she should go blank she could read the opening lines; she *could* read the whole address, but that certainly wasn't the way she wanted it. She wanted all of them to be proud of her, particularly her friends among the students and those close to her—T. I., Marguerite, and Alice Fletcher and Frank who were coming from Washington.

She slipped out of bed and took her dress from the wardrobe to see if it needed any last minute pressing. When she and Marguerite had gone shopping for the material and the clerk had brought out a bolt of blue and white pin stripe, Susan had known at once that it was what she wanted. The blue reminded her of a bright Nebraska sky.

She held up the dress and stood looking at it in the early-morning light. "It's the prettiest dress I've ever had," she thought to herself. The floor-length skirt was full, and there were ruffles at the throat and wrists. "Thank you, Nicomi," she whispered. "I'll do my best for all of you today—today and always."

The dormitory was beginning to stir. Her

time of privacy was over.

All too soon it was time to dress for the commencement exercises. Marguerite plaited her sister's shining hair into two smooth braids, and Susan bound them around her head. Where the two heavy braids crossed above her forehead, they stood up like a coronet. Then she stepped into the new striped dress.

Before she knew it, she was sitting on the platform with all the dignitaries, her hands clasped in her lap to stop their trembling. Her eyes searched the audience. In an instant she had found T. I., then Marguerite, and then Alice Fletcher and Frank.

When General Armstrong rose and strode to the podium, Susan's knees began to shake and the folds of her skirt started quivering. The General gave a short address of welcome, then announced a musical number. She didn't hear the song, but she knew when it was over, for the General was on his feet again. She was next.

As the General started his introduction, Susan began silently repeating the opening lines of her speech. But when Miss Patterson reached over and touched her hand, she listened to the General. "We have received word," he was saying "that our salutatorian has been awarded admission to the Woman's Medical College of Pennsylvania, where she will pursue the required studies to become a doctor."

The room broke into deafening applause. It

was as if the students were expressing their joy and pride with their hands. It went on and on.

Finally the General raised his hand for silence. "We indeed have reason to be proud. Susan is the first graduate of Hampton to be admitted to a medical school and the first Indian to be admitted at the Philadelphia college. I give you our salutatorian, Miss Susan La Flesche, who will speak on the subject 'My Childhood and My Womanhood.'"

Susan rose from her chair and approached the podium. Her heart was pounding. Her throat was dry. Would she be able to utter a word?

She turned her head toward the group on the platform, however, as she had planned to do. And yes, the words were coming from her throat: "Honorable Ladies and Gentlemen..." Her speech was launched. Her voice grew stronger as she faced her audience and continued.

It wasn't a long speech. It was plain and without pretensions. It came from her heart. And so her audience listened and they heard. They would have listened to anything she might have said, but they listened spellbound to this simple message of faith and work and hope for it spoke directly to them all; they heard and understood.

She could scarcely believe that she had finished, yet she had. The applause broke out again. She bowed to them, her friends, and smiled at them, then took her seat. Her part was over. Now she could sit back and enjoy the rest of the program—or so she thought.

But to her amazement, General Armstrong, back at the podium, turned toward her and was saying, "Susan, will you please come forward?"

Puzzled, Susan stepped to his side.

The General turned toward the audience. "I believe most of you know," he said, "that at Hampton we give a gold medal to the person passing senior examinations with the highest average. This year that honor goes to Miss Susan La Flesche." He held out a blue velvet box. "Susan, we are happy to present to you this symbol of your scholastic achievement. Congratulations."

Susan was stunned. First the announcement of her admission to medical college, then her speech, and now this. She stood with humble, modestly lowered eyes, very close to tears. Through trembling lips she thanked him, then slipped again to her seat. It was like a dream, all of it.

CHAPTER XV

Exciting Challenge

Susan found it hard to believe—as she and Marguerite once more boarded the westbound train—that this was good-bye to Hampton and the well-ordered campus life in which her place was secure, and good-bye to Thomas Ikinicapi in whose love she reveled. When she went East again in the fall, she would be entering a new and untried world.

There was a challenge in this that excited her, but it was dulled by the longing for the love that she had finally renounced. "I'm going to try to forget both past and future, and just enjoy my summer at home," she thought.

But she was to find this difficult. Her family would not let her forget her future, and her heart would not let her forget Ikinicapi.

"We are very proud," her father said. "You are a worthy daughter of the La Flesche name. You will do great service to our people as a doctor." Rosalie too was vocal, and, though her mother was silent as usual, her eyes spoke eloquently. All of them were taking her future as a fact.

"But I don't know if I'll ever be a doctor," she responded. "I don't know if I'll be able to master the courses in medicine. All I can do is try."

Father nodded his head. "If you try, you will win," he said simply.

"He sounds like T. I.," Susan thought. She knew that the whole road ahead of her would be a difficult one: first, mastering the work required to become a doctor; then, if she succeeded in that, practicing on the reservation.

The attempts she had made in previous summers to introduce ideas of cleanliness and sanitation had met with little success. Yet these were a basic part of any health program for her people. She would try again this summer.

"I'm going to visit every family in our village," she told Rosalie, "and, if I don't run out of time, I'll go beyond to the other village. I'll try to do two things: one, I'll try to get the women to wash their hands before they prepare food and everyone to wash before eating, and, two, I'll try to get each family to lime their privy."

"A big order," Rosalie commented. "But many know now that you're going to be a doctor. That should help."

It was a delight to ride her pony again, but some evenings she came home discouraged to the point of tears. "They look at me like they think I'm crazy," she told Rosalie, "when I talk to them about germs."

"Not all of them," Rosalie said gently. "Ed was at Wajapa's house today at noon, and he said the whole family was lined up at the pump to wash. 'Dr. Susan says wash hands before eating,' Wajapa told him."

Susan laughed. "Dr. Susan," she repeated. "Oh, Ro, do you suppose I really will become a doctor some day?"

"Of course you will."

Suddenly Susan became silent, her eyes on Rosalie's children who played in a patch of sunlight on the floor.

Rosalie saw and understood. She went to Sue and put her arm around her. "Yes, Little Sister, you are giving up a great deal to help our people."

"I want it so much, Ro," Susan said very low," all that you have—love and a home and children."

Rosalie held her sister tight for a moment, and Susan felt tears hot against her eyelids.

"Of course I knew summer would end, but not so soon," Susan said plaintively the day she began getting her clothes in order to go to Philadelphia. She had received a number of official-looking letters during the summer: one from the Bureau of Indian Affairs, stating that they would furnish $167 toward her fees at the medical college, and one from the Connecticut Indian Association, saying their organization was assuming the remainder of her expenses.

"This can't just be falling out of the sky into my hands!" Susan exclaimed on receiving word from the Connecticut Indian Association. "I think I see Alice Fletcher's influence in this."

"Yes," Rosalie smiled. "She's written me about what she's been doing to help you."

Susan shook her head. One of her big worries about medical school had been finances. Now this problem seemed to have been resolved. "People are so good to me," she said.

The most recent letter to have arrived was from a Mrs. Talcott in Philadelphia saying she would meet Susan and help her get located in a boarding house if she would let her know when she planned to arrive.

The remaining time at home flew by on swift wings. Soon Susan was again approaching the little wine-red depot that was the starting point of her trips East. She was as excited as she had been when Susette had bought tickets to Elizabeth for her and Marguerite.

She was still thinking about this as she boarded the train and waved good-bye to her loved ones. The train whistled, then made a great belching sound, and the wheels began to turn.

"I'll miss the family as much as ever," she thought, "and these beautiful hills, and the wide sky. But parting doesn't bring the feeling of desolation it once did. Perhaps it's because I'm a grown woman."

Susan noticed another difference. People no longer stared at her on journeys as if she were some strange wild creature. Instead, they looked at her with interest, sometimes admiration. Was it simply because she was better dressed than formerly? No, it must be more than that. Her years of education had made a difference. She knew that she now carried herself with a certain poise and assurance born of many things: the acquisition of knowledge, the experience of love, an understanding of herself, and her decision in regard to her future.

The journey through the browning cornfields and golden stubble fields of the Midwest, on into the wooded hills of Pennsylvania, and finally across the Susquehanna seemed surprisingly short. There had been so much to think about!

But as the train pulled into the outskirts of Philadelphia, Susan's mind was absorbed wholly by the sights and sounds around her. This was a huge city! The evidences of industry were on every hand. The smokestacks, the clang of steel on steel, the factory whistles, all amazed and excited her.

When the train pulled into the station, she realized that her heart was beating a quick tattoo against her ribs. Once again she was entering a new life.

Mrs. Talcott was pleasant and businesslike. "I've found a place for you in a boarding house just two blocks from the college," she said.

The next few hours were a blur to Susan.

Instead of a streetcar ride, she found herself riding in style in a hansom cab, its driver perched behind his passengers on a high seat overlooking the top of the cab. The spirited white horse between the shafts took them speedily to their destination. There her trunk was unloaded, introductions were made, and she was shown to her room.

It was almost time for the evening meal. Susan was introduced to a dozen men and women, some young, some middle-aged, some old, but her mind seemed unable to cope with fixing names to faces. She was glad when the meal was over and she could get back to her room, remove her clothing, and get to bed.

She was rested the next morning, and, after asking directions to the medical college, she stepped out into the crisp autumn day with her head and her hopes high. In her purse was the name of Professor Rachel Bodley, the person she was to see. "She knows about you and will see to your registration," Mrs. Talcott had said.

When Susan located the proper office, she saw that there were at least a dozen young women there before her. She stopped just inside the door, thinking to wait her turn. But the woman behind the desk looked up, laid down her pen, and went directly to Susan. "Miss La Flesche!" she exclaimed, seizing Susan's hands. "We are so very pleased to have you with us!"

"I am very glad to be here," Susan replied.

And indeed she was. Once the registration was over—a process not difficult for Susan with her fees already paid and the freshman courses all prescribed—she went with the others into a room where the class of 1889 was officially welcomed. To her surprise she was again singled out.

"We wish especially to welcome Miss Susan La Flesche from the Omaha Indian Reservation in Nebraska. Miss La Flesche was recently graduated with honors from Hampton Institute and comes to us with the highest recommendations."

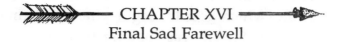

CHAPTER XVI
Final Sad Farewell

"Oh, I'm so very lucky," Susan thought one morning a few weeks later as she stepped off the porch of the boarding house and walked briskly toward the college. "Everyone is *so* good to me!" She had enjoyed a substantial hot breakfast, a pleasant "good morning" from each of the other boarders, a pat on the shoulder from the landlady Mrs. Smith who poured her a cup of coffee, and a bit of agreeable conversation at the table; and now she was going to classes, every one of which she found absorbing.

As much as she loved it all, however, Susan was homesick. Walking to the college, she warmed herself with thoughts of how she would spend the dollar Mrs. Talcott had given her for spending money to brighten her family's Christmas at home.

Christmas would be here before she knew it. Already the crisp autumn mornings had turned damp and bone-chilling, so that she hurried to get inside the building where her first class met. This class was anatomy, and it was her favorite. She was eager to get beyond textbook and lectures, and get into the lab work where she would see how the muscles were formed, layer on layer; how the arteries fed them; and all the rest.

Some of the students felt squeamish about dissection, which would begin after Christmas vacation, but Susan was looking forward to it. "We're so wonderfully made!" she thought as she stepped into the classroom. "Every baby that's born is a miracle."

She had been wondering how she would spend her Christmas vacation. Longing to go home but knowing that she couldn't, she supposed she would spend the time studying. Perhaps she would see some of the sights of Philadelphia. So far, she hadn't had time for them.

Then came a wonderful letter from Marguerite. Every letter she received was a joy, but this one proved to have news that sent her bounding to the kitchen to share it. "Mrs. Smith! Guess what? I'm going to Hampton for Christmas. Isn't that wonderful?"

"If that's what you want, I guess it's wonderful," Mrs. Smith said. She had been kneading bread dough; now she stood with hands poised over the pan. Her eyes narrowed, but they were twinkling. "Couldn't be you have a young man back there at Hampton?" she asked.

Susan tossed her head and laughed. "Could be!" she said. She wondered, as she ran up the stairs with her letter, how much of her excitement was due to her knowledge that she would see T. I. They had not been writing. She had received one letter from him after her arrival in Philadelphia. She had answered but had said plainly that she would be too busy with her studies to keep up a correspondence. T. I. had not replied. She had thought it would be unfair to give him hope. It would be better for him if he found another girl at Hampton, she told herself. Yet she had watched the mails for weeks, her heart sinking in disappointment each time she found no letter from him.

Now she would see him, she thought as she threw herself into a chair by the window and read Marguerite's letter from beginning to end. Miss Patterson and some of the other teachers, her sister wrote, had thought it would be very nice if Susan could come back and visit them. So they had taken up a collection for her fare, if she would come. Miss Patterson would write her, but she had given Marguerite the privilege of sending the news. Susan would surely come, wouldn't she? Then Marguerite answered a question Susan had asked in her last letter: No, T. I. was not going with any other girl.

Of course Susan would go to Hampton! The minute she received Miss Patterson's letter, she would accept.

The coming weekend she would go shopping for her family's Christmas gifts. Should she get T. I. something too? Her better judgment told her she should refrain—but wasn't Christmas a time for joy and giving?

The next day there was again a letter for her, but it was from Rosalie rather than Miss Patterson. And the news it contained was far from joyous. Their mother, Rosalie wrote, was very ill. Rosalie was doing her best to take care of her, but she really didn't know what to do. Mary's feet and legs were so badly swollen that she couldn't walk. She was running a high fever and was even delirious at times.

Susan turned at once to her books to see if she could diagnose her mother's trouble. She spent most of the evening writing to Rosalie, telling her what she had found. "I don't know how good this diagnosis is at long distance," she wrote, "but I think I have found the seat of her trouble." When she had finished the letter, she went to her bureau and took out the dollar bill she had been saving for Christmas. She held it for a moment, debating. Then she went back to her desk and added a postscript to her letter. "I am sending my dollar that I intended to use for Christmas. Please use it to wire me if Mother gets worse. If she improves, use it to buy meat. I am sure she needs protein in her diet."

She was so worried about her mother that it was difficult to keep her mind on class lectures that week. The letter from Miss Patterson arrived, and Susan answered it immediately, expressing her gratitude and accepting "unless something serious should happen at home." She went on to explain, "My sister Rosalie writes that our mother is very ill."

Near the end of the week, Susan received a letter from Rosalie. She tore open the envelope frantically, and her eyes scanned the page for news. She was so busy reading that she didn't notice a dollar bill falling from the letter.

As she read, her whole body relaxed. "Thank goodness!" she breathed. Rosalie had followed her prescribed treatment, and their mother was much better. They all appreciated Susan's sending the dollar, but Ro was returning it. Their government allotment was due, and Father would get meat for their mother.

For the first time since Susan had entered the medical college, the days now seemed to drag. She was already packed and ready to go before classes were dismissed for the Christmas recess.

She caught the first train out after school closed. It wasn't a long ride to Hampton, but she could scarcely contain her impatience to have it over. By the time the train pulled into the station she was beside herself with excitement. Would T. I. be there to meet her? Her eyes searched the crowd on the platform. Yes! He was at the foot of the train steps. As she stepped down from the train, he took her bag, and the smile he gave her made her heart turn over. Marguerite too was there. She threw her arms around her sister. "Oh, Sue! I thought the time would never come!"

Susan greeted Miss Patterson and the others who had come to meet her. Then she returned to T. I. As they left the depot he walked proudly at her side, just as he used to do.

When they reached the campus and crossed to Winona Hall, it was almost as if she had never left. The others faded away, and only Marguerite and Charlie were left in the parlor with Susan and T. I.

"Do you like it—medicine?" T. I. asked.

"Oh, yes, T. I., I do. I've known for a long, long time that I wanted to become a doctor, so my studies are like a dream coming true."

She saw the shadow cross his eyes, but he said, nodding his head, "I know you like it. That is good. But I am so glad you have come for Christmas. I miss you."

It was a long speech for T. I. It brought tears to Susan's eyes. "I miss you too, T. I.," she said, her voice choked. "I miss you very much."

The days of her visit sped by like birds in flight, and in no time it was Christmas Eve. It had been a beautiful, bright day, and she and T. I. had spent most of it together. When the early dusk fell and they went to the dining room for supper, the tantalizing aroma of oyster stew met them. "Oh, what a special treat!" Susan cried. It seemed to fit in with the rest of her day. "Perfect" was the only word she could think of to describe it. And upstairs on Marguerite's bureau was a little box that she was looking forward to giving T. I. later in the evening. Her heart had won out, and she had stretched her dollar to include a small gift for him. There was to be a midnight service. Before they went to it, she would give him his present.

She dressed with care for the evening. She was no longer wearing her hair in a braided coronet but in a soft upswept style called a pompadour. When she had finished dressing, she pirouetted before Marguerite. "How do I look?" she asked.

"You look very nice," Marguerite said, "but you'd be beautiful to T. I. if you were wearing moccasins and your hair was in braids down your back."

Susan laughed, knowing it was true. With the little box warm in her hand, she went down to him.

The ardor of his gaze as he watched her descend the stairs into the parlor was almost too much for her. She stumbled on the last step. Instantly he was at her side, catching her in his arms.

"Awkward!" she chided herself, laughing to cover her feelings.

T. I. steered her to a far corner of the parlor. "You are very beautiful," he said softly. They sat side by side on a sofa, and for a moment he looked deep into her eyes. Then he reached behind him and drew out a package. "For you, little Sue," he said.

"Oh, T. I., I have something for you too. But shall I open this first?"

He nodded.

The instant she saw what lay inside the box, her eyes misted. "Oh, T. I.! They're lovely! Beautiful! You made them?" Her voice broke.

"I made them for you, yes."

On her lap lay a pair of beaded moccasins. Her hand caressed them. "They're soft as a baby's skin. And so beautifully made."

"I shot the deer myself," he said proudly, "and tanned the hide."

"Did you bead them too?"

He nodded his head.

"I'll treasure them always, T. I.," she said in a voice that didn't sound like her own.

To break the tension, she reached into her pocket and brought out her gift for him. "It's nothing, compared to yours," she said.

But T. I.'s eyes glowed as he opened the little box and saw the lapel pin on its satin bed.

"The horseshoe is for good luck, T. I., for the best of luck always."

He took the pin out and fastened it in his lapel. "I will wear it *always*—over my heart," he said.

The moment was far too poignant for words. She thought she couldn't bear it. She reached for his hand, and, fingers entwined, they rose silently and went for their coats.

Through the star-spangled night they walked to the chapel. How many times had they gone this way before! But would there ever be another time? Susan thought the service the most beautiful she had ever attended. All the way through it she struggled with tears. She was affected by the familiar surroundings where she had known so much happiness, the soft light of the flickering candles, the lovely words of the Christmas story, the sonorous sounds of the organ, and T. I. at her side.

He did not go to the train with her the next day. To both of them their silent good-bye the night before as their hands clung together had been their final farewell.

It was difficult for Susan to get back into the routine of classroom and study. Pictures of T. I. kept flashing before her eyes, whether they were turned unseeing on a lecturing professor or riveted blindly on the page of a textbook. The occasions on which she had caught despair in T. I.'s eyes were the hardest to block out.

Before she left Hampton, Susan had been offered a teaching position there for the summer. On the surface this looked like the obvious solution for the summer months, for she could not afford to go home, and the job would furnish needed income. But, Susan thought, she could not afford to go back to Hampton if T. I. were there. How could she keep her mind on her work if he was close at hand? What a dilemma!

She had less and less time to feel sorry for herself as the term progressed. First there was her work, which grew increasingly interesting. Then there was her social life, which opened up a whole new world.

Shortly after her return from Hampton, the anatomy class moved from the classroom to the laboratory, and dissections began.

"This is our big day, is it not?" the Japanese

student, Mrs. Kei Okami, said to Susan as they started toward the lab.

Susan nodded. "Isn't it wonderful," she said, "to have this opportunity?"

Her companion smiled. "You have so much of the—how do you say?—enthusiasm!"

Susan laughed. Then she turned her attention to the professor.

"There is a cadaver on each table," he explained. "Six of you will work at a table. The body is divided into six parts. Two of you will be assigned to the head this morning, two to the chest, two to the abdomen. We'll get to the other three parts later. On subsequent days you will exchange so that each of you will have an opportunity to learn firsthand about all the parts of the body."

Susan felt excitement welling up in her. She clutched the little case that held the scalpels. This would be her first time to use one on a human body.

Susan took her assigned place. The laboratory assistant removed the sheet that had covered the cadaver. Susan heard a little involuntary gasp or two from her companions. She glanced at her partner and saw that she had paled and was biting her lip. "It's funny," Susan thought. "I'm not nervous, and I don't feel squeamish. I'm just so anxious to see how we're put together."

There was another phase of her work that

she also found enthralling at this time—surgical observation. The first time the class went to Clinic Hall she was amazed. The hall was in Woman's Hospital, and it reminded her of a huge theater. "I had no idea," she breathed to the student next to her. She watched enthralled as a patient was wheeled into the arena below and placed on the operating table. The anesthetist and the doctors were robed and ready. She watched them wash up. "And masks!" she thought. "If only I can get them to understand back home about germs and infection!" She looked at the instrument tray at the doctor's hand. Tomorrow she would be issued her own set of instruments! Oh, it was wonderful—too good to be true.

That night Susan wrote Rosalie in detail:

Today we watched two operations. They were performed by Dr. William Keen, one of the finest surgeons in the country. He is a very small man, but his reputation is enormous. First he took a tumor as big as a small apple from a girl's neck. He did it in about ten minutes. It was wonderful. The other operation was on a tiny baby. Oh, Ro, it is so marvelous that I am having this opportunity to learn to do the things that I want most in the world to do!

The next day Susan went to Dr. Keen to be issued her own surgical kit.

"Miss La Flesche!" he exclaimed. "Do you know I am so glad to see you here? I am so very glad indeed, and you are most welcome at the college. You know you are the first woman of your race to come here. And you plan to go back and practice among your people?"

Susan, embarrassed by her unexpected welcome, nodded.

"We are very glad to have you here," he repeated.

"You are most kind," Susan said. "I will try my best to become a good doctor."

"You will be a good doctor," her replied. "We know of your quick mind and your dedication. They are a proper combination."

When she came bouncing into her boarding-house after this encounter, Mrs. Smith called to her.

"How did you know it was me?" Susan demanded, going to the kitchen.

"Ho! A step like that! How could it be anyone else? You walk as though every step were taking you someplace you can hardly wait to get to!"

Susan laughed. "You know, that's exactly the way I feel, Mrs. Smith."

Mrs. Smith looked at her. "I wish I had half the energy you have," she said. "Well, there's a Miss Heritage that's been trying to reach you on the telephone."

"Who? Oh, yes, Heritage. I met them at church last Sunday."

When Susan first came to Mrs. Smith's, she had been afraid of the strange box on the wall with its raucous ring and the crank that had to be twisted. But she was used to the telephone now and turned to it with no fear or hesitation. When she had finished talking, she called to Mrs. Smith, "I'm sorry, but I won't be eating your good Sunday dinner. I'm invited to the Heritages' house after church."

The next Monday morning she had much to share with her friends. "I had the loveliest day yesterday," she told anyone who would listen. "I was invited to the Heritage home for dinner. They live in the most wonderful house I've ever been in. The floors are polished till you can see yourself in them. And the china and silver and glassware at the table! I tell you it was something to see—and flowers even! Flowers on the table in the dismal month of February!"

On the way to Clinic Hall, walking with Mrs. Okami, she said with a little laugh, "Do you know they had silver finger bowls at this place where I went for dinner yesterday. I didn't know what they were for, but I watched the others and did what they did. Oh, my! Little Sue from the Omaha Reservation, where they do well to wash their hands in a washpan before a meal—me, using a finger bowl!"

"You learn much beside doctoring here, no?" Mrs. Okami replied with a smile.

As the days and weeks went by, Susan thought often of this remark, for she continued to learn and to experience much besides medicine. The Heritages frequently invited her to their home. They introduced her to their friends, and there were more invitations. She met other cultured families at church and through the Connecticut Indian Association that was sponsoring her. She was quick to pick up the manners and ways of these new friends. And through them her horizons were ever widening. She was taken to concerts and the theater; she was invited to fashionable weddings; she went with her new friends to art museums and lectures.

"Who would ever believe," she wrote Rosalie, "that I would hear the world famous Madame Pattie sing, which I did last night? Oh, Ro, it was marvelous! What a voice she has. And all the bright lights. What a contrast to the lightning bugs at home! I do wish you could share this with me. Don't you think you could manage to come back for a visit in the spring?"

Later she wrote of her enjoyment of the opera *The Mikado*. "It was so cute! The darling Japanese costumes, and the choruses—Oh, I just can't describe it. It was heavenly." Susan also attended symphonies and a performance by the famous English actress known as the Jersey Lily.

121

"That's what they call her," she explained in her letter home. "Her real name is Lillie Langtry."

Nearly every weekend there was a new experience for Susan. The cultural feast came almost faster than she could absorb it—almost, but not quite.

"It's all adding to my womanhood," she told herself. When she thought of T. I., she thought of him with gentle compassion. The sharp pain had lessened to a dull ache.

CHAPTER XVIII

Citizen At Last!

Susan remained immersed in her studies and her social life, associating with colleagues and friends who were almost exclusively of the white race. Sometimes the Indian world—from which she had come and to which she planned to return—seemed far away. But in February, when the city lay wrapped in an unattractive gray winter shroud, something happened that brought her native world close, turning her thoughts to her people and making her feel proud to be an Indian.

Despite her busy schedule, Susan had been making observations at the outpatient clinic in Woman's Hospital almost every day. She found the time spent at the clinic the most rewarding of her day. "It's medicine in action," she had said to one of her colleagues.

As she was leaving the hospital one afternoon, Miss Garner, a fellow student who was walking with her said, "Have you read the papers?"

"No, I haven't had a minute," Susan replied. "Why?"

"Well, as I understand it, you are now a citizen."

"What?" Susan asked, puzzled.

"The Dawes Act passed, and, as I am sure

you know, it includes a clause giving the Plains Indians citizenship."

Yes, how well Susan knew! After all, wasn't that a part of what her sister Susette had been lecturing for? How her father would rejoice! Now her people would be able to go into the courts and get compensation for wrongs done them. She thought of the two thousand dollars her father had not been able to recover from a white trader he had trusted, money that he needed desperately for his family.

The women talked as they walked. "I can hardly believe it," Susan said, shaking her head, "after all these years. How I wish I could be home when Father hears the news."

Being on the reservation to rejoice with her family would have been the best of all ways to celebrate the good news. But Susan did receive a phone call from Frank.

"How do you like being a citizen?" her brother's voice boomed.

"Oh, Frank, isn't it wonderful? Father..."

"Yes, I'm so glad he lived to see the day. Of course not all our people are happy over some of the provisions of the Dawes Act."

"No, some won't like having the land divided up."

"But, Sue, we're wondering if you could spare a little time this weekend? We thought we might come down and celebrate."

"Of course I'll spare the time. Who's 'we'?"

"Susette and Tibbles and Alice and I."

"Oh, good! Alice too."

"Yes, she's as happy as any Indian!"

Susan laughed. "Good for her. Are we going to celebrate with a pow-wow?"

Frank's laugh at the other end of the wire warmed Susan's heart. Usually she thought he, like her father, took life almost too seriously.

Before the party from Washington arrived, Susan had relayed her news to a friend, Mary Tyndall, whom she had known at Hampton and who now taught at the Lincoln Institute, an Indian school just outside Philadelphia.

"Bring your family out," Mary urged Susan. "We'll help you celebrate. The students would be so thrilled to meet Bright Eyes."

As Susan turned from the phone, she smiled, thinking how she once would have been jealous that Susette had been singled out. Now she was only proud. "I guess the difference is that I've found my niche in the world now. It won't bring me fame, but it will bring me satisfaction."

On Saturday morning there was a knock on her door. She called, "Come in," and the door burst open.

"Susette!" she cried, running to her sister and throwing her arms around her. She pulled her into the room. "How good to see you! Where are the others?"

"Downstairs. I wanted to have you to

myself a few minutes. I wanted to find out—but I can tell by looking at you. You're happy in medicine, aren't you?"

"Oh, yes, I love every minute of it. I'm just impatient to finish so I can get back to the reservation and begin work."

Downstairs, with greetings over, Susan told them of Mary Tyndall's invitation.

"Fine!" Frank said. "I've been wanting to visit the Lincoln Institute. Let's go!"

As they set out, Susan walked with Susette and Tibbles. Alice Fletcher and Frank followed. Suddenly a stab of longing pierced Susan's heart. How nice it would be, she thought, if they were *all* walking two-by-two, T. I. at *her* side.

But when they reached the Institute and Mary came bounding to meet them, Susan's good nature returned. After introductions had been made, Mary turned to Susette and said, "Oh, Bright Eyes, we're so proud to have you with us. Won't you speak to the students?"

Tibbles gave a vigorous negative shake of his head in reply. "She's worn out from speaking," he said.

But Susette said, "I could say a few words."

Tibbles frowned in disapproval but said no more. Susan and Frank exchanged a glance that said, "Good for our sister. She isn't letting Tibbles take over."

When the students were assembled, Mary said proudly, "I want you all to meet some very

126

important people. You know Miss Susan La Flesche who has been here before. I want you to meet her brother Mr. Francis La Flesche, who works for us in the Bureau of Indian Affairs. And another important guest from Washington is Miss Alice Fletcher, who is studying the customs of the Omahas. And Miss Susan's brother-in-law Mr. Thomas Tibbles, who has lectured and written widely in behalf of our cause."

Susan thought, "If she doesn't go on fast, *he'll* make a speech. He never misses an opportunity."

Mary, however, did not pause. "And our special treat, Miss Susan's sister Bright Eyes, who is going to say a few words to us," she finished.

As Susette stepped before her young audience, Susan found that her own eyes were smarting with tears. This was her sister who had found the courage to stand before many audiences in order to help her people.

"Boys and girls," Susette was saying, "did you know that something very important to all of us happened recently? A bill was passed by the United States Congress that granted citizenship to many Indians. This of course makes us happy. But let me remind you that with privilege comes responsibility. We must be *good* citizens."

"That was perfect," Susan whispered to her

as, amid loud applause, she rejoined the others. Then Susan herself was on the spot. She realized Mary had spoken her name, and Susette was nudging her.

"I said *you* would say a word," Mary said, laughing.

Susan had never considered speaking to be one of her strengths. When she had spoken before audiences, she had always prepared carefully. To be asked to speak extemporaneously was frightening! There she stood with all those eager eyes on her, and she hadn't an idea what to say. But her sense of humor came to her rescue. She giggled just as she and Marguerite used to giggle as girls.

"She really caught me, didn't she?" she said. "I was whispering, and now I have to take my punishment!"

They all laughed.

"You see," she went on, "I'm not a speaker like my sister Bright Eyes. I'm just a student like you. I'm studying very hard to become a doctor so I can take my place as a responsible citizen. And the most important thing *you* can do is study hard and get an education. Then you will be prepared to be responsible citizens also."

CHAPTER XIX

Practicing Medicine Too Soon?

As spring came on and summer vacation drew near, Susan's longing to return home became intense. The summer job at Hampton had been confirmed, so she knew she would not see Nebraska for at least another year. It seemed an eternity. She thought with nostalgia of the previous summers she had spent at home.

"With all my new friends, and loving my work as I do, you'd think I'd be satisfied," she chided herself. But still the longing remained—the longing to see her dear ones, the longing to jump on her pony and ride with the wind, the longing for the feeling of freedom that the wide countryside and the big sky gave her. "I guess I'll never get over it," she thought. Then she laughed at herself, for she would be going back to it all, to spend the rest of her life where she could see a million stars in the black sky at night and hear the wild geese honking spring and fall, where the sunsets blazed in golden glory and faded to melon and mauve. Oh, her lovely country!

Before it was time to leave for Hampton, Susan received a letter from Marguerite assuring her that she needn't worry that T. I. would be there. He was leaving at the end of the spring term, not to return. Susan sat staring at the letter. It was a relief, of course, to know she would not be thrown with him again, for she didn't think either of them could go through another parting. But what would Hampton be without him?

She was soon to find that it was haunted with ghostly memories and was less than stimulating. Fortunately she enjoyed the teaching more than she had anticipated; at least she was being helpful to people who badly needed help. Yet she was impatient to have it over so she could get back to her medical studies and her friends.

Getting back to her medical studies was as satisfying as she had anticipated. She had to tell Rosalie about it. She wrote:

Dear Ro,

I'm beginning to feel as if I know a little bit about these wonderful human bodies we're blessed with, a little about how they operate and what makes them go wrong, and best of all, a little about what to do to help set the wrongs right.

Will you please send me the symptoms whenever someone's ill at home? Then I'll see if I can diagnose the case. It is so important that I be able to do this, for a doctor must understand what is causing pain or fever or other symptoms, before he can treat the patient effectively.

Rosalie's reply to this letter made her chuckle. Ro hadn't lost either her sense of humor or her common sense! "The most obvious 'symptoms' I see around here," she wrote, "are Father's stumbling with that wooden leg of his and rubbing the stump. What is your diagnosis, Madam Doctor? I know what mine is—also what I would recommend as a cure!"

Susan knew well what she meant: Father needed a new wooden leg!

"Your diagnosis, also recommended cure, confirmed by Dr. Sue," she wrote back. "I'm sending most of the money I earned this summer. (I kept a little for some small presents for you at home and my dear friends here when Christmas rolls around.) I hope this is enough to get Father a new peg leg. But do see that he goes to Lincoln and gets a proper fitting. His trouble with the one he has stems from inefficient handling of his care and careless work in fitting him."

It wasn't long until another letter from Rosalie gave in detail the symptoms of a disease that was plaguing Wajapa. Susan studied them with care, checked with her books, then drew up her diagnosis and followed it with her recommended treatment.

"Will you please check me on this?" she

asked her friend Mrs. Okami, handing her the sheet she intended to enclose in a letter to Rosalie. "It's for my sister on the reservation. She wrote me the symptoms..."

Susan got no further.

"What are you doing?" her friend asked in surprise. There was a note of apprehension in her tone. "It is very frowned upon to practice medicine before you are a doctor."

Susan was taken aback. It had never occurred to her that she might be doing anything wrong. She was merely eager to begin helping her people and, she admitted to herself in all honesty, to test her own knowledge.

"Oh, I—I'm not practicing medicine," she stammered. "My sister just sent me these symptoms and asked what I made of them. This was my diagnosis."

Mrs. Okami continued to read from the sheet Susan had handed her. She frowned. "But you are also recommending treatment," she said, "and that you must not do! If they found out, they—they might—how do you say—remove you from medical school."

Susan paled. She reached for the offending paper and tore it to bits. "Oh, Mrs. Okami!" she said. "Thank you very much. I guess—it was very foolish of me. I just didn't realize."

After that she saved her diagnoses for the hypothetical cases in the textbooks. But they seemed very impersonal compared to Wajapa's gout and the other medical problems of the people on her reservation. There was another whole year of training after this, and this one was not half over.

But the months went by, and, before she knew it, examinations were coming up again. The tests were scheduled for early March, to be followed by a twelve-day vacation.

Susan studied hard. Still she felt some uneasiness when she went into the first examination in advanced chemistry. "Imagine me being nervous over an examination!" she thought. She had always enjoyed being tested. Quickly she scanned the questions. When she had finished her perusal, a little smile played on her lips. The questions were much easier than she had anticipated.

Next came anatomy. "I studied just the right things!" she thought exultantly.

When Susan reached her boardinghouse, there was a letter for her. "From Frank!" she exclaimed. She tore it open and scanned it quickly. "Oh, wonderful!" she cried, running to share her good news with Mrs. Smith. "My brother's coming to visit me!" It would be the first time she'd seen any of her family for nearly a year.

When Frank arrived at Mrs. Smith's door, Susan greeted him with admiration, "Oh, Frank, you're so handsome!"

"You're looking very handsome yourself,

Little Sister," her brother said. He shook his head. "Doctor Sue!" he said in wonderment.

Susan laughed. "Oh, no! Not yet. I still have fifteen months to go. That's a long, long time. And, Frank, sometimes I think I just can't stay away from home that long. It seems forever."

"You'll make it," he assured her. "But while I'm here you're going to forget work. We're just going to have a good time. What do you want to do first?"

"Oh, I don't know. There are so many things I want to see."

"Have you been to Independence Hall?"

"No. Isn't it awful when I've been here a year and a half?"

"And we'll see what's playing at the opera."

"And my friends want to meet you and entertain you."

The days and the evenings went all too fast. Soon it was Frank's last day. They had saved Independence Hall until then because there was a parade scheduled to go past the Hall that day. They stood in the crowd waiting for the parade to come into sight. The music of the approaching band made Susan tingle. When the flag bearers and drummers came around the corner, she cried, "Don't they look splendid?"

As the band came abreast of them, she stood on tiptoe straining to see what would follow.

"Oh, Frank, look!" she cried. "Indians!"

Frank began to laugh. "Make-believe ones!" he said.

They were still laughing as they made their way with other tourists to see the Liberty Bell. But when they reached the front hall of the boardinghouse, and she stopped to pick up her mail, her laughter was instantly stilled. A yellow envelope addressed to Miss Susan La Flesche and bearing the frightening word "telegram" stared up at her.

"Oh, Frank!" she whispered, turning pale. She stood holding the envelope in her hand, making no move to open it.

"Do you want me to open it?" Frank asked.

Susan nodded. She watched his face as he tore open the envelope and read the message. His face was grave, and he didn't speak.

"What is it?" she breathed.

"Nicomi," he said.

"Is she—is she..." Susan couldn't bring herself to say the word.

"Yes," Frank said. "She died in her sleep."

Susan was very glad that Frank was with her when she received the news of Grandmother Nicomi's death. It was the first break in the family within her memory, and it was difficult for her to accept.

"Oh, I wish I could go to them!" she cried. Then, ruefully, she added, "And we were so happy just a little while ago."

"That's life, Little Sister," Frank replied gently. "You'll have to accept that if you're going to be a doctor."

After Frank had left the next day, she was very lonely. "Another whole year before I can be back with my dear ones," she thought, "and then it won't be the same, with Nicomi gone."

Almost immediately she began urging Rosalie to make plans to come East. "Come sometime before I leave," she wrote her. "It would mean so much to me, and, after all you've been through, you owe yourself a vacation."

But the only reference Rosalie made to her plea was to write that if she were to come East, it would be the following year, to be present when Susan received her degree.

"They're really depending on me," Susan thought as she read this. "What if something should happen and I wouldn't graduate?"

But that school year ended and the next began—and nothing had stopped her headlong progress.

"I'll wager you have the highest average in our class," Mrs. Okami said to her one day.

Susan laughed aloud. "I don't know about that," she said, "but I know it sounds funny to hear you say, 'I'll wager.'"

Susan thought about what her Japanese friend had said. Her grades were good, she knew, but she didn't work for grades. She worked to learn all she could possibly learn. Sometimes it frightened her to think she would be entirely on her own when she went back to the reservation, with no one to ask if a diagnosis were correct or if one prescription would be better than another.

She mentioned something of this to her surgery professor one day as they removed their masks following a tonsillectomy at which Susan had assisted.

"You are so *sure*," she said. "I wonder if I will ever be. When I think of being on my own..."

"You will be quite all right, Miss La Flesche," he interrupted. "I have no fears regarding your competency."

"I appreciate your saying that," Susan said as they walked out of surgery together, "but, when I begin my practice, I will have no one with whom to consult."

"I understand you are going to practice on the Omaha Reservation."

"That is my hope," Susan replied. "There is great need. It's difficult to explain, but having to adjust to a whole new way of life has resulted in many problems for the Indian, among them, serious health problems. That's where I hope I can help."

"Your task will be difficult, but I am sure you will meet the challenge."

"Thank you for having faith in me. I will try to live up to it, if and when I become a doctor."

The doctor smiled as they parted. "I would say you can remove the 'if,'" he said.

Susan smiled too, but there it was. For some reason she could not explain, she continued to insert an "if" in her thinking. And before her senior year had progressed far, something happened that made her "if" very real.

It came in the form of a yellow envelope again, a yellow envelope waiting for her on the hall table of her boardinghouse. This time she must open the envelope and face its contents alone. She managed to tear it open. The telegram was from Rosalie again, and Susan knew even before her eyes could send the message to her brain that it was bad news.

She sank into a chair and reread the cryptic telegram message that said, "Father took bad cold Stop Went into pneumonia Stop Condition critical Stop Ro"

Just one thing kept pounding through her mind: "I have to go. I have to go." But somehow her legs would not obey her brain's command to be up and on her way. She just sat and stared at the yellow paper in her hand. Finally she steadied herself on the table and pushed out of the chair.

She climbed unsteadily to her room, pulled out a suitcase, and began throwing clothes into it. "I have to get money," she thought. She did not think of her medical knowledge or of what might be done for Iron Eye. She just kept numbly repeating: "He's going to die. It isn't fair." Tears streamed unheeded down her face as she packed. "He won't get to see me graduate," she sobbed.

The next few days were always to remain a blur to Susan, a gray, rain-streaked—or was it tear-streaked?—blur. Somehow she got herself together. She called the Heritages and asked for a loan. She wired Rosalie that she was coming home. Then she phoned the dean of the college to say she was leaving, but she scarcely heard when Dr. Bodley asked, "Are you sure it is wise, Susan, to leave your classes like this?"

"I'm leaving on the evening train," was all she could say.

By the time she had done these few necessary things, Miss Heritage was there with

139

money. Seeing Susan's distraught state, she said, "I'll go to the train with you."

The train couldn't begin to carry her home fast enough. She dozed fitfully, only to waken from one bad dream after another, each involving her father: He was falling off a high bluff as she ran toward him, unable to make her legs go fast enough to reach him in time to save him.... The reservation agent was taking his house and land away from him, and he stood desolate and alone.... And then the worst one of all, the one from which she wakened sobbing: Father was coming to her commencement exercises, walking stiffly with his wooden leg, but proud and erect. Just as he entered the hall he fell, and he did not get up.

As she stepped from the train at long last, her eyes searched the familiar depot platform for Rosalie. But Rosalie was not there. Rosalie's husband was.

"Ed! How is he?" she demanded as he reached her at the foot of the train steps.

She saw him wet his lips, saw the solemnity of his face, and she knew.

"He's—he's gone, Sue. He died about ten thirty last night."

Susan heard, but she could not accept her father's death. "He can't be gone," she whispered. "My medical degree. He hasn't seen me get..." Then she crumpled in Ed's arms.

CHAPTER XXI
Head Of The Class

In the days that lay ahead, Susan went about in her private gray mist of grief. She was like a sleepwalker, going through the motions of dressing, of cleaning the house, of greeting friends, of attending the funeral.

When it was all over, Rosalie asked, "When do you plan to go back, Sue?"

"I don't know."

"You shouldn't miss any more of your classes than you have to," Rosalie said gently. "Much as we like to have you with us..."

"I don't know that I'll go back," Susan said woodenly.

"Not go back?!" Rosalie demanded in shocked amazement. "What do you mean?"

"I wanted Father to see me get my degree. I wanted him to see me come back here and start helping his people."

"Of course you did," Rosalie said soothingly. "But he knew you were going to make it. He was so very proud of you, Sue."

"It doesn't seem worth the effort now."

"But it *is* worth the effort. It's more important now than ever," Rosalie said. "Sue, you're just not yourself or you wouldn't talk this way. Maybe you do need a few more days before you go back."

In the week that followed, Susan remained bitter and aloof. She went off on long rides on her pony, looking for solace in the hills she loved. But nothing seemed to help.

Then one day things changed, and it was not the hills but the people that had roused her. Back from her ride, she strode into her mother's kitchen with her old self assurance. She was glad to see that Rosalie was there.

"You know Little Elk's grandson, Thomas?" she said, almost before she was through the door.

"Yes," Rosalie said, nodding.

"You know he and his wife have a baby about a year old?"

Again Rosalie nodded. She had helped deliver the baby.

"Well, would you believe that baby has rickets? Of all things—*rickets!* And not because he doesn't get enough to eat but because he can't tolerate cow's milk, which his mother has been trying to feed him. And because she's kept him shut up in that dark house with the blinds drawn—never taken him into the sunlight even for a minute. The mother said she thought the sun would hurt his eyes!" Susan stopped and stood with hands on hips, shaking her head. "What these young mothers don't know!" she ended.

"So Dr. Sue prescribed sunlight and what? Goat's milk?"

"Exactly. Only don't 'Dr. Sue' me yet. I still have eight months to go."

She saw the relief in the glance that passed between her mother and Rosalie, and she smiled back at them. A couple of days later she boarded the train for Philadelphia.

As her senior year progressed, she began thinking about the mechanics of her practice-to-be. One could not just go home and start practicing medicine on the reservation. Everything that was done there had to be done under government regulation. She wrote Frank about it. "Can you set the wheels to rolling? I don't have any idea how to begin."

Frank soon replied that he and Alice Fletcher were working on the problem of getting her set up on the reservation. "As if it should be a problem," he ended.

Her weekly letters home were getting shorter as end-of-term pressures grew heavier, but in every one there was reference to two things: her eagerness to return home and her desire for Rosalie to come to commencement. "You simply must come," she wrote Rosalie. "I can't graduate without you. It's hard enough knowing Father won't be here. We seem such a little family with him and Nicomi gone."

To her delight a letter finally came saying that both Rosalie and Marguerite were coming for her graduation. This was more than she had dared to hope for!

Marguerite was teaching in the reservation school. She and Charlie had been married the winter before, and Susan had cried because she couldn't go home for the wedding. They'd had a church wedding, something very new for the Omahas. Marguerite had patterned it after one she and Susan had attended when they were at Hampton.

So much had happened, Susan thought, in the years since she had been away: births and marriages and deaths. Her family had gone on without her. "They might have waited for me," she thought wryly. But that wasn't life. Life moved on, and she'd better get moving with it. The last examinations were looming in the weeks ahead. And already there were matters to be taken care of in connection with graduation.

As the final weeks sped by, a letter from Frank interrupted Susan's headlong progress and caused her more than momentary concern. So far, he wrote, neither he nor Alice Fletcher had been able to cut through the red tape that would set up Susan's practice on the reservation. "We'll be down to see you graduate, never fear," he ended.

Impatiently Susan tossed the letter on her bed. What would her graduation amount to, what good would the three years of hard work be, the years of separation from her family, the sacrifice of love, if she were not to be allowed to help her father's people—*her* people?

But final examinations were upon the class of '89, and, worries or no worries, she must discipline her mind and see them through to the best of her ability.

Finally they too were over. Grades were in. There remained only the formalities of commencement.

The joyful anticipation of seeing Rosalie and Marguerite overshadowed all else, and she could scarcely contain herself as she waited for the train that would bring her two sisters, her brother, and Alice Fletcher into Philadelphia. Rosalie and Marguerite had gone first to Washington to meet the others, and they would all arrive together.

When at last the train pulled into the station, Susan could see only dimly the beloved group waving to her from the window. Tears had filled her eyes to overflowing.

"Oh, Ro! Marg!" she cried, flinging her arms around them almost before they were off the bottom step. Holding her two sisters and being held in their embrace was like being home.

She broke away to greet Alice Fletcher and Frank, laughing through her tears. "It's good to see you. It seems so long!"

As they moved happily along the platform, Susan said, "There are so many people I want you to meet—so many wonderful friends!

They're all coming to commencement tomorrow. I'll do my best to get you all together. There are thirty-six of us graduating—the illustrious class of 1889! I'd like you to meet all of them."

"Aren't you going to ask if you have a job waiting for you?" Frank asked her, half teasing.

Susan looked at him sharply. "You have news?" she asked.

He nodded. "Perhaps not exactly what you'd like to hear, but it was the best we could do."

"What? Tell me quickly!"

Her brother handed her an envelope. "It's all in there," he said. "You've been appointed physician to the government school on the Omaha Reservation."

Susan opened the envelope and read. No, it wasn't exactly what she had wanted. Still, if she could help the children.... Suddenly she realized that they were all standing there smiling at her, waiting for her to say something.

"Thank you, Frank and Alice. Without you I wouldn't have had this."

"Just think! You'll be home with us all—in just a few days now—home to stay!" Marguerite said.

"The appointment doesn't begin until September," Susan said, indicating the letter.

"But you're going home with us, aren't you?" Rosalie said quickly.

Susan knew by Ro's tone that she sensed

something had been left unsaid. "I—I'm not sure," she replied evasively. "Let's wait until after commencement tomorrow to talk about immediate plans."

Rosalie gave her a searching look but said no more.

The next morning was bright and beautiful. "It's a good omen," Susan thought.

Soon she was sitting on the stage with her thirty-five classmates, searching the audience for family and friends. As the exercises proceeded, her mind went back to other commencement exercises—at Elizabeth, and at Hampton. Thinking of Hampton brought memories of T. I. and a sudden stab of pain. Lost in her thoughts, she was startled when she heard her name called.

Susan saw that Dean Bodley had turned from the podium toward her. In some confusion, she rose and stepped forward.

"We have, in this graduating class," Dr. Bodley said, "an outstanding young woman, an Omaha Indian, the first woman of her race to become a doctor, Miss Susan La Flesche."

Applause broke out, but the dean held up her hand for silence. "This in itself makes us very proud here at Woman's College. The fact that Miss La Flesche plans to return to minister to her own people makes her story even more satisfying. But there is more: the climax, you might say." She looked at Susan, who was experiencing a mixture of emotions—happiness, embarrassment, bewilderment—and the dean's eyes twinkled. "The climax," she repeated, "of which even Miss La Flesche herself is not aware."

Susan's brows drew together. She had thought Dean Bodley was going to make the announcement that she was one of the six to remain and intern at the hospital that summer. But now there was something else, of which she herself was not aware?

"Of the thirty-six members of the class of 1889," Dean Bodley continued, "Susan La Flesche has consistently maintained the highest scholastic average, so that she graduates at the head of her class."

Now the applause broke out thunderous and long, and Dean Bodley made no effort to restrain it.

Susan's throat tightened. Her eyes sought Rosalie in the sea of faces below her. Even at a distance, she could see that tears were streaming down her sister's cheeks. "She's clapping for Father too," Susan thought, and she felt tears misting in her own eyes. "And there's still the announcement of my internship to come! Won't *that* set them back?" With this thought she was able to smile at the audience. "Smiling through tears," she said to herself. "Is this too an omen?"

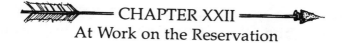

CHAPTER XXII
At Work on the Reservation

Susan's family was delighted over her opportunity to intern in a Philadelphia hospital. "After all," Rosalie said, smiling with pride, "you will be home to stay in just three months."

But in those months during which she spent long days at Woman's Hospital, she had no time to think of the days ahead. Every waking moment was crammed with work, with learning, with decision-making. The decision-making was always in collaboration with other more experienced doctors, but Susan checked herself closely in each case. Always she decided in her own mind what the procedure should be in a case before a decision was reached in consultation. She was preparing herself for the time when she would have no one with whom to consult.

Then at long last she was home! Home where she could feast her eyes on the rolling hills that sloped down to the curving river. Home where she could quiet her mind with the peace the long vistas always brought her. For the first time since her father's death, she came to know a measure of acceptance. He had loved these hills, this river; he had loved his people and devoted his life to them. She would pick up where he had left off.

"We will examine every child," she told the teachers in a meeting prior to the opening day of school, "and start a record for each. We'll work first with those having the most serious problems. For example, if there is a child whose vision is impaired, he cannot perform satisfactorily in school. We will see that he is fitted with glasses. If there is a child suffering from malnutrition, he will be too listless to learn. We will see that he gets proper food. Understood?"

They understood, Marguerite among them, for they had been well aware of the serious physical handicaps of many of their pupils.

Susan suggested that they start the examinations with the children in the upper grades and work down. "If they've been struggling with a physical handicap for twelve or fourteen years," she said, "that's long enough. The eighth graders first." She also suggested they be sent to her two by two, partly because she knew the Indian children would be fearful of a doctor and partly because she thought this procedure could save time.

On the first day of school Susan walked into the room that was to be her office, put down her little black bag, and looked around. Within the four bare walls there were only a desk, two straight chairs, and the scale she had requested. She sighed. "I'll have to get some pictures on the walls, some curtains at the windows, and a couch with a bright coverlet."

In a few minutes two big solemn-eyed boys stood at her door. As she smiled at them and said warmly, "Come in, boys," her quick eyes took in much: unkempt hair (she must teach them to wash their hair; teach them grooming; teach them pride), sallow complexion (diet— that was one of the biggest health problems on the reservation; she must educate the young about foods), poor posture (no wonder there was so much consumption; they stood round-shouldered and hollow-chested).

"Isn't this a nice morning to be starting school?" she asked brightly.

She received only grunts in reply, grunts that did not seem to agree with her enthusiasm.

"Well, let's see. Names first." She sat behind the desk and drew out two blank cards. Once she had placed the boy's name and age at the top of each, she began her examination. The card of the first boy filled rapidly. She began with height and weight. "At least I don't think they'll be afraid of getting weighed," she told herself. Then eyes, ears, teeth, heart, lungs. She kept up a pleasant patter of talk as she worked. But as she wrote: "Teeth badly decayed. Vision in right eye 20/40. Acne," she thought, "I'm afraid this is typical. How badly I am needed!"

By the time the day was over she was exhausted. Nonetheless, she took her box of cards home with her. She must go through them, pick out the ones that indicated children with the most acute conditions, and call them in the next day for treatment or referrals.

That was where her troubles began. Not with her own treatment—salve for open sores, kerosene for head lice, swabs for sore throats—but with the referrals. She would send a note home saying Jimmy must be taken to a dentist to have his teeth filled or Mary must be taken to an oculist to have glasses fitted. Each day she would ask Jimmy or Mary if he or she had been taken to town for the recommended work. And day after day she received the same answer: a negative shake of the head.

So she started riding her pony to the homes of these children after school to talk to the parents. Sometimes she was able to convince them of the need for the child's care and of the importance of good physical condition for the sake of the child's schoolwork and his entire future. Sometimes it took several calls before she succeeded. Sometimes she failed completely. But whether she succeeded or failed, Susan's visits convinced her of one thing. In order for the lot of the children to improve, their home life must be improved.

One evening she arrived at the home of a little first-grade girl whose eyes were so bad that Susan felt sure she could never learn to read. Her note home requesting that the child be taken to town to an eye doctor had received no response. Each day when she asked Jennie about it, she got the same reply, "My Mama's sick." When Susan asked, "Well, what about your father? Can't he take you?" she was met with a shake of the head.

Now as she dismounted and tied her pony, she gave the yard and the house before her a quick scrutiny. She shook her head at what she saw. "Just as I thought," she muttered. The yard was a shambles, full of what Susan mentally termed "junk"—a wheel here, a rusty tool there, a piece of broken farm machinery, an old churn, and a vast accumulation of bottles. "Um," Susan thought. "That's the father's problem, the bottle."

Jennie met her at the door, a shy little thing who kept her head down. "Mama says come in," she mumbled.

The interior of the room was dark. From the far side of it came a weak, fretful wail, and Susan saw that a woman and a baby lay on a rumpled bed.

"Come in, Doctor," the woman said. "I'm sorry I can't get up, but I'm so weak."

Before she departed, Susan had not only left medicine for the mother and baby, but had promised that she herself would take Jennie to an eye doctor the following Saturday.

She stopped by Rosalie's on the way home.

"You look tired," Rosalie said. "Sit down, and I'll get you a cup of coffee."

"I'm so discouraged, Ro," Susan said as she sank into a chair. "It just isn't going to do it."

"What isn't going to do what?" Rosalie asked, pouring coffee.

"My just being doctor to the children. Their problems stem from even worse problems at home. I should be the reservation doctor, not just the school doctor."

Rosalie looked at her sharply. "You seem to keep pretty busy the way things are," she said.

Susan gulped her coffee, straightened, and said resolutely, "I'm going to try. I'm going to apply for the appointment of reservation physician."

Rosalie just shook her head.

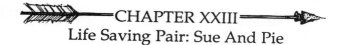
Life Saving Pair: Sue And Pie

Susan wrote a letter of application on the very night that she told Rosalie she wanted the position of reservation physician. Then she waited anxiously for a reply.

At last the letter arrived. She tore it open eagerly. "Well, finally," she sighed. She carried it to the kitchen where her mother was preparing supper. "I got the appointment," she said. "I don't get any more money though."

Her mother looked up. "So much more work and no more pay?" she asked.

"That's what the letter says: 'As there are no funds available except for your present salary as physician to the government school, we will be unable to pay any additional moneys for your additional services as reservation physician.' Well, anyway I have the title. Now to see what I can do with it."

That same night, the first snow of the winter fell. Susan was soon inundated with a siege of colds, grippe, and pneumonia. It was as if the first snowstorm had been a signal for winter illnesses to attack.

She had laid her plans carefully before entering into her new contract to do two jobs for the price of one. She would spend mornings at the school and would make house calls in the afternoons. The only problem, she soon discovered, was that there weren't enough hours in the day.

"I don't know why babies always want to get born in the wee hours of the morning," she said to Rosalie, stopping at her sister's house one day on the way to school. Susan had been up since midnight and would not have time to go home before she was due at school. She was glad to have a place to clean up and get a cup of coffee.

"Sue, you can't go on this way," her sister said. "You'll ruin your own health."

Susan sighed. "But what else can I do, Ro?"

It was a bad winter, one of the worst Nebraska had seen in many a year. The north wind blew in icy gusts, finding its way around poorly fitted window frames and under ill-hung doors into the Omahas' houses. Many of the houses were getting old, and they had not been kept in repair.

When Susan rode up to one in which a windowpane was out, the hole stuffed carelessly with old rags, anger flared in her. Inside, she knew, lay a child on the verge of pneumonia.

"Tom," she said, when she had entered, "there's no excuse for that." She pointed at the window. "When you get your next allotment, buy a piece of glass and some putty and replace that pane."

"You're just like Iron Eye," he said, and Susan detected resentment in his tone. "Always trying to tell us how to live."

Susan bit her tongue and went about her task of examining the sick child. Was it hopeless, she wondered, trying to teach them? But her father had never given up.

One morning when she started for school, the wind was particularly vicious. Reluctantly, she turned Pie into it. When they reached the schoolgrounds, she immediately put him into the shed that was provided for bad days. As she turned to the schoolhouse, she noted that the sky looked ominous. It took all her strength to wrench the door open against the wind. "I think we're going to get snow," she called to Marguerite as she entered.

Marguerite turned back, and Susan saw the worried look on her face. "Oh, dear, I hope not. Charlie's sick again. He has an awful cough, Sue, and he was so hot last night. I know he has fever. And he went out to look after the stock this morning. I was hoping you could go by and see him this afternoon."

"Of course I'll go. A little snow won't stop me," Susan replied with a smile, hoping to cheer her sister.

As the morning progressed, the wind howled and the snow grew heavier. In a moment's lull in her work, Susan glanced out the window and discovered she could no longer see the row of trees that formed a windbreak for the school building. She felt a little tug of concern. Some of the children lived quite a distance from school. Perhaps they should be getting home.

It wasn't long until the teachers were consulting her. "Do you think we should dismiss school? If it keeps this up..."

"I think it would be wise to get the children on their way. It certainly isn't getting any better."

So an early dismissal was agreed upon.

Susan was helping the teachers bundle the children into coats and overshoes, tying mufflers over mouths and noses, and giving instruction to the older ones to keep a tight hold on the hands of younger brothers and sisters, when the outside door burst open and a man stumbled in. He was so caked with snow that at first she didn't recognize him.

"Dr. Susan!" he cried. "Come quick! My Minnie..."

"Oh, it's you, Joe," she said. "Has your wife started labor?"

He nodded. "But she's bad, Doctor. Not like before."

"Come on in and warm up, then go home and put lots of water on the stove to heat. I'll be along shortly."

Joe didn't linger. As soon as the children were on their way and she had straightened up her office, Susan sought out Marguerite. "I'll have to wait to see Charlie until after I deliver

Minnie Whitefeather's baby. Joe says she's having a bad time, so I may be late."

"All right. Be sure to bundle up," Marguerite said. "It looks like the storm's getting worse."

"That I will. I always come prepared!" Susan assured her. She pulled her stocking cap down over her ears and donned the heavy wool mittens her mother had knit for her.

"I hope you'll be all right," Marguerite said. "It's a long way over there."

"Don't worry. You can depend on Pie!" Susan waved a cheery good-bye and plunged out into the storm. She had to fight her way to the shed. Already drifts were piling high. "I hope the children are all safely home by now," she thought. Her pony was nervous. "Good old Pie," she said, patting the sleek neck as she mounted. "When you were a young one and we went racing across the hills, you didn't think you were going to have to plow through all kinds of weather with me when you grew old, did you?"

The Whitefeathers lived on the northernmost edge of the reservation. Susan turned Pie onto the road, and he plodded into the storm. "Good boy!" she said encouragingly. But she couldn't hear her words above the violent shrieking of the wind. Nor, shortly, could she tell whether they were following the road; she could only trust Pie.

It seemed to her that the storm grew worse by the minute. Suddenly Pie stopped, turning his head back as if asking Susan what he should do. She tried to wipe the caked snow from her eyes to see what was wrong and found that her fingers were stiff. But she saw Pie's problem. A huge drift lay across their path. "We'll have to go around it, Pie." She pulled him to the left until they reached a point where the drift tapered off. Pie moved around it, and Susan thought, "Now can we find the road again—if we were on the road?" She pulled on the right rein. But she couldn't tell whether they were going north, for now the storm seemed to be swirling around them from all directions.

Soon another drift blocked their way. But this time Pie wallowed through with a strange, swimming motion. How did he know he could get through that one and not the other, she wondered. Suddenly, having maneuvered the drift, the pony stopped.

"Get up, Pie! We have to go on!" she urged. He did not move. She slapped the stiff reins on his neck, but to no avail. She tried kicking his sides with feet she discovered were numb. "We'll freeze to death! *Go on!*" Still Pie refused to move.

At length she dismounted. If she could walk on her numb feet, perhaps she could lead him. Stumbling, she made her way to Pie's head.

Then she saw, and she caught her breath in terror. For Pie stood with his head directly over a bundle in the snow—a bundle that she knew instantly was a child. "Oh, my God!" she cried. She lifted the bundle into her arms. It was a boy, one of the little ones they had turned out of school to find his way home. "What were we thinking of?" Susan railed at herself. "Jimmy! Jimmy!" she cried, shaking the child. She scooped the snow off his eyelids. He stirred, and then his eyelids lifted. "Jimmy! It's Dr. Sue. You were asleep, Jimmy. You have to wake up now." She hoisted him in front of her on the pony, and, holding him close to give him warmth from her body, she beat on his arms.

The minute she was back in the saddle, Pie moved on. "Pie! Bless you. You probably saved Jimmy's life."

As Pie pressed on, Susan continued to talk to Jimmy, working on him as she talked—rubbing his hands, cradling his face against her breast. "We have to warm up your nose," she told him. He began to cry. "You mustn't cry. Your tears will make cakes of ice!"

She strained her eyes ahead, but she could see nothing against the driving snow. She had no idea how long they had been in this frozen white nightmare. Surely, if they were going in the right direction, they should have reached the Whitefeathers' by now. "Pie's going to take us to where it's nice and warm," she soothed

Jimmy. And to herself she said, "If he doesn't, it's the end for all of us, you and me and him. And maybe Minnie Whitefeather and her child too."

She tried to keep Jimmy awake, finding to her consternation that she herself was growing drowsy. She well knew that to go to sleep was a sure way to freeze to death.

She must have dozed briefly, for she started when Pie suddenly stopped. She roused herself to urge him on. "Get up, Pie! We can't stop now! We have Jimmy!" She kicked his sides, but the pony refused to move. The snow had again caked her eyelids, and she pawed at it with unfeeling fists. She supposed they'd come to another drift Pie couldn't manipulate.

As she blinked hard to see, she was suddenly aware of a sound that was not born of the storm. Pie had whinnied. She even felt the ripple-like movement of his neck. What did it mean?

Then she saw! They were by the side of a building, sheltered from the wind. It was a barn!

"Pie! Pie! You did it!" she cried.

As she tried stiffly to dismount with Jimmy, strong arms were supporting her. It was Joe.

"We are so glad you're here, Dr. Sue. We were afraid you would not make it."

"So was I," Susan said. "Please take care of Pie. We wouldn't be here except for him."

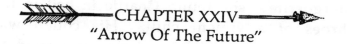
"Arrow Of The Future"

Susan delivered a baby girl that night, but she did not get to Marguerite and Charlie's. Nor did she get to her sister's home for the two days following, because the storm raged on fiercely through the night, wrapping the reservation in a tight white cocoon that could not be penetrated. There was no way to return Jimmy to his home or to let his parents know that he was safe. Susan agonized over this, but there was nothing she could do.

There were two other Whitefeather children, and Susan noticed that they came to have their hands washed before a meal. She noticed other things too: the family's clothes were clean, and so were the blankets on the beds. "You're doing well with your little family," she praised Minnie.

Minnie smiled. "Remember the summer you were home from school when you rode around trying to teach people to wash their hands before meals? We believed you—about germs and all."

"And now you're teaching your children," Susan said approvingly. "That's fine, Minnie. It means the upcoming generation will have a better time of it."

When Susan eventually got to Charlie and Marguerite's, she found Charlie in bed in the throes of a violent chill. His cough was frightening. She left medicine and tried to reassure him, but, as her sister saw her to the door, Susan shook her head. "His lungs are weak, Marg. You'll have to be very careful."

"I know," Marguerite replied quietly.

"I wonder if she does know," Susan thought as she went on her snow-clogged way. There was no question in her mind that Charlie was consumptive, as his mother had been. Susan had been doing all she could for him, but she feared he would be one she couldn't save— gentle Charlie, who was so good to everyone, especially to Marguerite.

By early February he was continuously confined to his bed, and there was no more Susan could do. Marguerite had to take leave from her teaching position to care for him.

He died quietly, as he had lived, just before the month was out.

"I thought maybe if he could make it till spring..." Marguerite said desolately.

"Why don't you come home and live with Mother and me?" Susan suggested. "It would be too lonely for you here."

They sent word of Charlie's death to his family in Dakota, and his brother Henry came. "We wanted the family represented at his funeral," he said.

"Henry's different," Susan remarked to Rosalie. "Yet he reminds me of Charlie. Sort of a more cheerful, livelier version!"

"He's more worldly," Rosalie said.

Susan smiled. Yes, it had taken Ro, who had had less "worldly" exposure than the rest of them, to see straight through to the point. "Yes, you're right," she agreed.

With the funeral over, Henry gone, and Marguerite back in the home where she and Susan had grown up, things settled down into a certain routine. Marguerite went back to teaching, and Susan went on with her doctoring.

"It's like the old days," Susan said one evening when she and Marguerite and their mother sat down to supper.

"Only different," Marguerite said.

"Yes," Susan agreed, thinking of how it had been when Nicomi and Iron Eye and Rosalie had all been at that table. "Things don't stay the same, do they, Mother?"

Her mother shook her head.

"We have to learn to accept change. That was one of the things Father tried to teach us long ago. And Frank has reminded me of it too."

Spring was late that year, but when it finally came, it was so beautiful that Susan at times thought she couldn't bear it. Sometimes when she was riding home from a call in early evening, she would dismount and let Pie graze while she gazed down on the greening of the willows that fringed the river like a band of chartreuse lace. If it weren't too late, she would venture into the woods to look for wild flowers—violets and Dutchman's-breeches and the shy lady's-slipper.

"What a wonderful place to live," she thought. And more and more she could see that her work was bearing fruit. "I'm not accomplishing miracles," she told Rosalie one evening, "but I am beginning to see some of the results of better hygiene and health habits. And we're losing fewer babies and fewer cases to infection."

"You don't need to convince me," Rosalie said. "I can see it on every hand. How pleased Father would be."

In early May, Susan received a letter from the Hampton Institute. It was an invitation to be the commencement speaker at the school the following month.

In the weeks that followed, she thought about what she might say to the Hampton graduating class. But before she had actually formulated her speech, news came from the reservation of the Dakota Sioux that blotted out all other thoughts. Thomas Ikinicapi was dead. She had not heard from him in several years and had no idea that his health had been failing. The news was a shock, and in the days that followed she could not throw off her grief.

T. I.'s death took the edge off her anticipation of the trip to Hampton. As she boarded the train for the East, she was subdued and sad. When she reached the campus, she felt even more depressed. Everywhere she turned, T. I. seemed to be walking at her side, as in the old days. A few of the same teachers were still at the school, but most of them were new. General Armstrong was ill, and she went to visit him.

"I'm going to be at commencement," he told her. "My doctor has given me permission." He indicated the wheelchair near his bed.

"Fine!" Susan said. "That will make it a real Hampton commencement for me."

"It's our twenty-fourth—a fine time to honor one of our most famous graduates."

"Famous? Me?" Susan laughed. "Plodding through mud and snow to deliver babies and quarantine houses with scarlet fever scarcely makes for fame."

"You've been written up in several journals, you know."

Yes, she knew, but that wasn't important. The important thing in her life was building a better future for her people.

On the day of commencement the sun was shining, and the world was glowing with the beauty of June. As Susan dressed in the new dress Rosalie and Marguerite had insisted she have for the occasion, she could smell the scent of mock orange through the open window. She could not throw off her mood of depression. "Mock orange!" she said aloud. The scent made her think of weddings. Indeed it mocked her!

They seated her on one side of the platform, along with General Armstrong in his wheelchair. "There's going to be a little pageant to introduce you," the principal explained to Susan. "We need most of the stage for it."

To Susan's surprise, however, when the exercises were ready to begin, General Armstrong wheeled his chair to the center of the stage and introduced the pageant with a single sentence. "The test of the civilization of any nation is the care that it gives to its oppressed classes." Susan thought about that. It had real meaning for her.

She watched with interest as the pageant began. A beautiful girl dressed as Columbia—an American flag draped about her, a crown on her head, and a staff in her hand—took her place center stage, symbolizing the United States. A chorus sang "Columbia, the Gem of the Ocean." Then students representing noted early Americans—William Penn, John Smith, George Washington, John Adams, and others—filed in to take their places at one side of Columbia. Following this, a young woman designated as "Indian Petitioner" threw herself at Columbia's feet and asked why her people were not represented.

Graciously, Columbia called in Pocahontas and Sacajawea who stood at her other side. "Only women?" Susan thought. "Are they doing this for my benefit?" But then Columbia began calling in Indian men, and in a moment, to Susan's amazement, there was one representing Chief Iron Eye of the Omahas. Susan was deeply touched.

When Columbia was flanked by the two races, a young man came front and center and said, "So has been America's past. What of her future?"

As he stepped back, another youth came on stage, went directly to Susan, and took her hand, indicating that he wished her to rise. Amazed that she was to take part in the pageant, Susan went with him to the center of the stage. When there, she saw that two other youths were coming toward her, one from each side. One carried a large bow, the other an arrow. The young man carrying the arrow placed it in Susan's hand as he said, "Dr. Susan La Flesche, arrow of the future." From her other side came the voice of the youth with the bow, "Shot from the bow of the past."

Susan's throat constricted. But she must not cry. Not here. Not now. Carefully she laid the arrow on the podium, and leaving her prepared speech until later said, "Thank you, both for my father and for myself. The name La Flesche does indeed mean 'arrow.' And if I can be an arrow that shoots into the future straight and true, I feel that I will not have lived in vain."

CHAPTER XXV

Susan La Flesche Picotte–M.D.,G.P.

La Flesche. The Arrow. Yes, Susan thought, as the click-clack of the train wheels ticked off the miles on her return trip from Hampton, truly the name La Flesche was symbolic. And the concept used at the commencement exercises—born in the mind of General Armstrong, but executed very well by the Hampton students—was valid. Frank, working in the Bureau of Indian Affairs; Susette, lecturing and writing; Rosalie, binding the two races and continually helping the Indians in a thousand ways; Marguerite, teaching in the government school; and she, herself, doctoring and teaching the rules of health and hygiene—they were all arrows shooting into the future.

The pageant, with the place the La Flesche name had in it, had lifted Susan's spirits so that when she arrived home she was again her usual energetic self, ready to tackle once more the task she had accepted as her destiny. To her surprise she saw, as the train slowed to a stop, that it was Marguerite who had come to meet her rather than Rosalie. And there was a young man at Marguerite's side. As Susan descended the train steps, she recognized him. It was Walter Diddock, who was employed at the government school to teach the boys farming.

Marguerite embraced her sister, and Walter Diddock put out his hand. "Good to see you back," he said.

"How was it?" Marguerite wanted to know. "Do tell us all about it."

Walter took Susan's bag and led the way to a shiny black buggy with a sleek mare between the shafts.

"Oh, what a nice rig!" Susan exclaimed. "Is it new?"

"Yes," Walter said, looking at Marguerite, "I thought anyone as pretty as your sister deserved a nice buggy to ride in."

Susan smiled at Marguerite, whose eyes were lowered demurely. So that was the way things were! Walter was courting Marg. Well, that was good. He was a fine young man, and Marguerite was too young to remain alone. And what of herself? She wasn't exactly old! Suddenly the years ahead stretched very long.

The summer and fall saw Walter Diddock's buggy making frequent trips to the La Flesche home. Susan watched her sister depart in it evening after evening, to return in a rosy glow.

One day when spring was again upon the land and the young couple had gone out, Susan said to her mother, "I don't think it will be long now." She was glad of her sister's happiness, but once again, as when the two of them had first gone away to school, she found herself having to fight a little feeling of jealousy. She

172

among all the sisters was to be left to face the world alone.

All during her second winter as reservation physician, she had continued to drive herself to the limit of her strength, taking care of both her jobs. Her mother and sisters protested, but she did not heed their pleas to reduce her working hours, to refuse to make house calls except for serious cases, and to spend less time and energy demonstrating proper health habits.

She didn't resent the long hours she put in and the time spent on house calls, for in the homes she had her best opportunity to teach. And more and more, the results were showing. Still, with all hours full and with the satisfaction of a job well done, she was restless. If she was looking peaked, as Rosalie and Marguerite insisted she was, she thought it more due to not being at peace with herself than to overwork.

When Marguerite announced her engagement, Susan admitted something of her feelings to Rosalie. "Of course I'm glad for Marg," she said. "And I'm so glad you have Ed and the children, Ro. But I guess I'm a little bit jealous."

"Your work isn't enough then?" Rosalie asked sympathetically.

Susan shook her head. "It should be, I suppose. I wouldn't give up my work—not for anything."

"What you're saying is that you'd like a

home and family too," Rosalie said.

"I guess that's it," Susan agreed.

But soon her mother fell ill, and, with the added responsibility of caring for her, Susan had little time to think of herself.

One evening in May she was riding home at sunset, feeling less tense than for some time, since her mother seemed to be out of danger. "Another spring!" she thought. "How the seasons do come and go." Spring always brought Susan a special surge of pleasure. As they rounded the bend that brought home into view, Pie suddenly threw his head up and gave a quick snort.

"Now what's the matter with you?" Susan asked in surprise.

Then she saw. A man who must have been sitting beside the road had jumped up and startled the pony.

"Hello there!" he called.

Susan reined up. "Why, Henry Picotte!" she exclaimed. "I didn't recognize you at first. What are you doing in this part of the country?"

"Waiting for you at the moment. I've been with a Wild West Show down South, and I decided I'd had enough of that life. So when we came north, I left them in Omaha."

"Do come home with me and have supper with us."

"I'd be happy to." Henry smiled warmly at her, and, to her surprise, Susan's heart did a flip-flop. As he walked beside her pony, they continued to talk easily together, and suddenly for Susan the spring took on a new dimension. It was the usual symphony, but now she was a part of it.

In the days that followed, the symphony rose in rapid crescendo.

"You're good for me, Henry," Susan said one evening as the two of them sat on the porch steps listening to the whippoorwills calling and the frogs croaking. "I don't know when I've laughed so much."

"I'm glad if I'm good for you, Susan," Henry said softly, reaching for her hand, "because I'd like to spend the rest of my life with you."

Susan gripped the fingers that held hers. "And I with you, Henry. But you'd have to understand that I couldn't give up my work."

"I do understand. I know it has to be that way with you. I'll find work here, better work than being with a show."

When the hour grew late and the little night sounds were all but stilled, Henry left her. Susan tiptoed softly up the stairs so as not to waken her mother and went to Marguerite's room. "Marg," she whispered, "are you awake?"

"Hmmmm," Marguerite murmured sleepily.

"I just wanted to tell you yours isn't the only wedding coming up. Henry and I are going to be married too."

"Sue!" Marguerite cried, wide awake in a flash. "Oh, I'm so glad for you!"

The sisters talked until the dawn light was breaking. "Just like old times," Susan said when she finally started for her own room.

As she undressed, she thought again of the pageant at Hampton. As clearly as on the day the words were spoken, she heard them now: "La Flesche, arrow of the future, shot from the bow of the past." A future worthy of the past, she hoped: a better day for her people, helped by her work; and another family of the La Flesche blood, born of her union. This continuity—past, present, future—was what made a person one with the earth.

Epilogue

Susan La Flesche Picotte's work as a physician continued for many years. After she and Henry married in 1894, they lived for a time in the town of Bancroft. Although Bancroft was on the Omaha Reservation, its population was made up of both whites and Indians. Susan doctored them all. At night she placed a lighted lantern on her doorstep to guide those anxiously seeking a doctor.

Her hope for a family was fulfilled with the birth of two sons, Caryl (born in 1895) and Pierre (born in 1898).

Henry died in 1905, and the next year Susan moved to the new town of Walthill, which had been founded in the center of the Indian population. Here she built a tall house just across the street from Marguerite and Walter. Over the mantle, she placed a brass plate bearing the words: "East, west; home's best." Always, her home was very dear to her.

From the days of her early work on the reservation, she had dreamed of a hospital to serve the area. After years of hard work on her part, a hospital was finally built in Walthill, and for a few years she had the opportunity to work in a modern medical center.

After her death in 1915, the hospital was named the Dr. Susan Picotte Memorial Hospital.

Bibliography

More information on Susan La Flesche or Susan Picotte can be found in the following sources:

Avery, Susan and Linda Skinner. "The La Flesche Sisters," in *Extraordinary American Indians.* Chicago: Children's Press, 1992.

Diffendal, Anne P. "The La Flesche Sisters: Susette, Rosalie, Marguerite, Lucy, Susan," in *Perspectives: Women in Nebraska History.* Lincoln, Nebraska: Nebraska State Council for the Social Studies/Nebraska Department of Education, June 1984 (Special Issue).

Ferris, Jeri. *Native American Doctor: The Story of Susan LaFlesche Picotte.* Minneapolis: Carolrhoda, 1991.

Green, Norma Kidd. *Iron Eye's Family: The Children of Joseph LaFlesche.* Lincoln, Nebraska: Nebraska State Historical Society/Johnsen Publishing Co., 1969.

Waldman, Carl. *Who Was Who in Native American History: Indians and Non-Indians From Early Contacts Through 1900.* New York: Facts on File, 1990.

Research materials can also be found at
The Nebraska State Historical Society Archives—Lincoln
The Medical College of Pennsylvania (formerly the Woman's Medical College of Pennsylvania)—Philadelphia
The Picotte Center (formerly the Dr. Susan Picotte Memorial Hospital)—Walthill, Nebraska

Index

*Note: The Female Medical College of Pennsylvania changed its name, in 1867, to the Woman's (which has often been misspelled as Women's) Medical College of Pennsylvania. The college was affiliated with the Woman's Hospital of Philadelphia (also often misspelled as Women's). In 1970 the college again changed its name, this time to the Medical College of Pennsylvania.

About the Author

Marion Marsh Brown is an award-winning author with eighteen books and numerous magazine and newspaper articles to her credit. Her most recent awards and honors include the Y.W.C.A.'s Tribute to Women, 1991; the Peru State College [Nebraska] Distinguished Service Award; the Nebraska Library Association's Mari Sandoz Award, 1993; the Humanities Association's Sower Award, 1994; the Synod of Lakes and Prairies (Presbyterian) Outstanding Senior Nomination, 1993; and an Honorary Doctor of Letters, Peru State College, 1995.

Ms. Brown is a life member of the prestigious Nebraska Writers Guild. She lives in Omaha, Nebraska, and is currently at work on another young reader's biography and an adult novel.

Books by Marion Marsh Brown

Young Nathan (1949)

The Swamp Fox (1950)

Frontier Beacon (1953), reprinted as *Stuart's Landing* (1968)

Broad Stripes and Bright Stars (1955)

Prairie Teacher (1957)

Learning Words in Context (textbook, 1961; revised 1974)

Silent Storm (1963), with Ruth Crone

A Nurse Abroad (1963)

Willa Cather: The Woman and Her Works (1970) with Ruth Crone

Marnie (1971)

The Pauper Prince (1973)

The Brownville Story (1974)

Only One Point of the Compass: Willa Cather in the Northeast (1980) with Ruth Crone

Homeward the Arrow's Flight (1980), excerpts used in Open Court K-6 Reading Program text, Level 4:1, unit on medicine (1995), book revised and reprinted as **Homeward the Arrow's Flight: The Story of Susan La Flesche** (1995)

Dreamcatcher: The Life of John Neihardt (1983) with Jane Leech

Sacagawea (1988)

Singapore (1989)

Susette La Flesche (1992)

ORDERING INFORMATION

Homeward the Arrow's Flight

The true story of
Dr. Susan La Flesche Picotte
(Omaha Indian)

If you local bookstore is unable to obtain
this book, you may order directly from:

FIELD MOUSE PRODUCTIONS
RECORD PRINTING COMPANY

1-800-658-3241

or Mail to:
Record Printing Company
PO Box 540
Cairo, Nebraska 68824-0540

We Accept Visa & MasterCard